DYNAMIC
ART
PROJECTS
FOR
CHILDREN

Includes Step-by-Step Instructions and Photographs

DENISE M. LOGAN

CrystalProductions

Glenview, Illinois   Aspen, Colorado

Library of Congress Cataloging-in-Publication Data

Logan, Denise M.
  Dynamic art projects for children : includes step-by-step
instructions and photographs / Denise M. Logan.— 1st ed.
      p. cm.
  ISBN 1-56290-350-0
  1. Art—Study and teaching (Elementary)—Activity
programs. I. Title.
  N350.L55 2005
  372.5'044—dc22
                                    2005026500

ISBN 1-56290-350-0
Printed in Hong Kong

TABLE OF CONTENTS

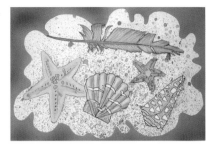

elements and principles of design: design is a concept that refers to the plan or organization of an object in the environment – the arrangement of independent parts to form a coordinated whole. Design is achieved through the use of elements and principles.

ABOUT THIS BOOK

These art projects are a collection of art lessons that were created and taught in the Gilbert, Arizona public elementary schools and successfully completed by thousands of children in 1st through 6th grade with phenomenal results.

Creating art opens a window into a child's imagination. These projects facilitate the creation of a beautiful piece of art by tapping into creativity as well as build confidence and self-esteem.

Dynamic Art Projects for Children excites and empowers children to use art as a positive avenue for self-expression.

TO PARENTS

Children need to learn how to utilize their creativity and express it in a constructive way. Children thrive on your encouragement and praise. Your interest and participation in these art projects lets your child know that their thoughts and feelings are important. Each child's creation is unique and becomes an extension of themselves — a way of defining who they are.

ABOUT THE PROJECTS

Dynamic Art Projects for Children takes a how-to approach. Each project provides step-by-step photo guidelines that eliminate confusion and supply a clear vision of the desired results. Children enjoy these projects because there is a defined goal that gives them direction yet is still open ended enough to allow for their own creative approach. This focus actually enhances creative results.

Children also respond because familiar materials are used in new and interesting ways.

TO TEACHERS

Art is an effective vehicle for assimilating new knowledge in all areas of classroom curriculum. *Dynamic Art Projects for Children* is an effective resource in the classroom because the step-by-step photos make it easy to use at a moment's notice and the required materials are basic. Each lesson has reference to concepts and topics that connect to subjects such as art elements and principles, skills, appreciation, history, and culture and related topics such as science, math, and literature.

THE LANGUAGE OF ART

The language of art consists of line, shape, color, texture, pattern, and form. These work together like words to make visual sentences. The brainpower to combine thoughts, feelings, and information into a visual sentence is an important communication skill. Even though the solutions are limitless, it is not disorganized thinking; rather it is developing the ability to organize and redefine elements into an aesthetic whole. Refining this creative problem solving skill benefits all aspects of life.

CRAZY CACTUS

CONCEPTS

ELEMENTS: LINE, SHAPE, COLOR
PRINCIPLES: RHYTHM, TEXTURE

When a single line bends to touch itself or another line, a shape is created. Repetition of bending lines that connect and build upon each other in a progression from large to small creates a visual rhythm that, like rhythm in music, is a unifying force for the overall composition. These two basic concepts are the foundation for this playful and even humorous cactus project. Cactus plants are fascinating in their many varieties. Descriptive phrases like zig and zag, wiggly like Jello, flat like a pancake, skinny like spaghetti, purple with polka dots, help open a child's imagination to the wild possibilities as they draw, color, and "texturize" a "crazy" cactus. Squeezing paint from a bottle and adding colorful bits of paper is an exciting twist to this project.

MATERIALS

12 x 18-in. white construction paper or sturdy drawing paper
Pencil
Scissors
Water-based markers and/or watercolor paints
8½ x11-in. colored paper (in <u>bright</u> colors)
3 to 5 narrow-tipped dispensing bottles
  (sources: perm solution bottles found at beauty supply stores, mustard or catsup dispenser bottles with a fine tip, or dispenser bottles from craft stores or art catalogs)
"Squeeze Paint" or fabric paint

Squeeze Paint Recipe:

1½ cups water
⅓ cup salt
1¾ cups flour
3 teaspoons MSG
  (preservative-optional)
1-2 tablespoons liquid or
  powder tempera paint
  for each bottle

Directions:

In a blender combine all ingredients except paint, into a thick, smooth milkshake-like solution. Pour equal portions into 4 or 5 bottles about two-thirds full. Add paint to each bottle, replace nozzle, and shake well. Adjust water, flour, or paint as needed. Note: If the solution in the bottle becomes too thin with time, add a little Wondra® flour and shake. (Wondra® comes in a 13.5 oz. blue canister and is made not to lump when added to liquids).

line: the path of a point moving through space; it can vary in width, direction, curvature, length, and even color.

shape: shape is an area that is contained within an implied line or is seen and identified because of color or value changes. Shapes have two dimensions, length and width, and can be geometric or free-form.

color: visual sensation dependent on the reflection or absorption of light from a surface; hue, value, and intensity are the three main characteristics of color.

rhythm: the regular repetition of particular aspects of a design.

texture: the surface quality of materials, either tactile or visual.

1. Draw cactus.

On a 12 x 18-in. piece of white art paper, draw curving lines in various sizes and shapes that connect and stack on top of each other. Start with the biggest shape at the bottom and progress upward.

2. Make cactus needles.

Cut three or four sheets at a time of the colored paper into strips that are about one inch wide. Then cut these strips into triangle shapes by making diagonal cross cuts.

3. Color and/or paint cactus.

Fill in the drawing with imaginative colors and designs using markers and/or watercolor paints.

4. Add "squeeze paint" and paper needles.

Shake bottle and gently squeeze to test paint for right consistency on a separate sheet of paper first, then rest nozzle on the drawing surface and outline the cactus, a section at a time. Poke paper needles into each wet section of paint. It will harden and hold them in place. Work away from wet areas to avoid smearing fresh paint.

Tip
Clogged nozzle tips can be cleared with a pipe cleaner or a straightened paper clip.

STUDENT WORK AGES 8-10

ABSTRACT CITYSCAPE

Klee, Paul (1879-1940). *Castle and Sun*, 1928. Canvas. Private Collection, Great Britain. Photo Credit : Erich Lessing / Art Resource, NY. © 2005 Artists Rights Society (ARS), NY / VG Bild-Kunst, Bonn

CONCEPTS

ABSTRACT ART
CITYSCAPE
ELEMENTS: SPACE

When artists create pictures of a city, called a cityscape, they usually begin by thinking about the basic lines, shapes, and colors they will use to communicate this city experience. If the artist is more interested in general ideas rather than exact details, the art might be more "abstract" in style. In abstract art, the artist does not attempt to represent the world exactly as he sees it but rather to convey what he knows or feels about it.

Swiss artist Paul Klee created an abstract cityscape called *Castle and Sun* in 1928. Notice his use of many geometric shapes to create this cityscape.

This abstract cityscape project incorporates only simple rectangular shapes and basic dots and lines. The color choices, style and placement of shape and line all become the tools that create the mood or feeling of this cityscape. Each child's creation invariably takes on a personality of its own. Transparent tissue paper buildings create new and unexpected colors as pieces overlap. Children enjoy this process of discovery.

MATERIALS

12 x 18-in. sheet of construction paper
(yellow, light blue, orange, light green, gray, tan, or pink)
Tissue paper (nonbleeding assorted colors)
Scissors
Soft round paint brush
Liquid starch
Small bowl
Squeeze paint (recipe: see Crazy Cactus project, page 7)

1. Assemble supplies and cut tissue paper.

Layer different colors of tissue paper together and cut several at a time in simple rectangles or any building shape you desire.

Tip

More starch is needed under the tissue if it separates from the surface as it dries.

abstract art: art which depicts subject matter with simplified or symbolic forms.

cityscape: a picture representing a view of urban elements, such as buildings.

space: expanse in two- and three-dimensional art which we describe in terms of height, width, and depth; the object or the picture plane is divided into positive space (the object itself) and negative space (the surrounding area).

2. Adhere tissue shapes using starch and a brush.

Begin at the top of the construction paper and adhere tissue shapes by brushing an area with starch and laying tissue on the wet patch and brushing over the top. Overlapping and varying placement of tissue will create a feeling of space. (Shapes near the bottom of the paper appear to be closer than shapes placed closer to the top.)

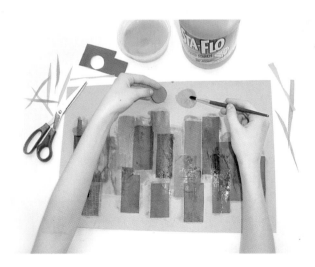

3. Add atmospheric details.

Sun, moon, haze, or cloud shapes are cut from tissue and adhered in the same way.

4. Add structural details.

Rest the nozzle of the squeeze paint on the damp and/or dry surface and "draw" around each building. Add lines and/or dots to the inside of buildings for windows and structural details.

Tip

If needed, mist and press the dry project under books to flatten any curled edges.

STUDENT WORK AGE 8

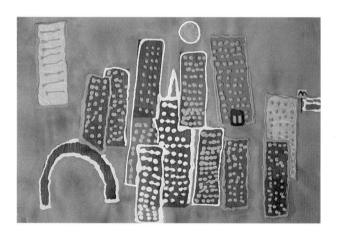

FANTASY SPACE ART

Robert T. McCall, *Within Our Reach*. Courtesy of the artist. www.mccallstudios.com

CONCEPTS

ASTRONOMY
FANTASY SPACE ART
ILLUSTRATION TECHNIQUES

Artists who specialize in this style of fantasy art combine art and science in an exciting hybrid that requires the skill and precise work of traditional fine art. Planetary maps and knowledge of the planets, stars, and endless wonders of the universe are as necessary as a palette and brush to these artists. Good "space art" makes the viewer want to go there. NASA employs this art form to further the space program as you can see on the left.

In this project, art and science combine to portray scenes of places you have never been and will never see. Techniques, using nontoxic materials, have been adapted for the classroom to create galaxies, comets, exploding stars, domed cities, space rocks, crevices, and planets.

MATERIALS

12 x 18-in. black construction paper
12 x 18-in. bright white construction paper
Liquid tempera paint (in various colors)
White tempera paint
Soft round paint brush
Old toothbrush
Spray bottle of water
Black oil pastel
White chalk
Pencil
Scissors
Glue sticks or clear gel glue (not pictured)
Circle templates or round objects to trace
Fine white iridescent glitter
Posterboard pieces
Plastic wrap (not pictured)
Ruler

1. Spatter white paint on black paper.

Place paper in the center of a covered surface. Dip toothbrush into the white paint and flick a fine spray of paint by brushing thumb over bristles. Create larger dots by tapping a brush with paint against a pencil.

Tip
Any accidental "blobs" of white paint can be covered up later with a planet.

2. Make planet paper.

Spray a sheet of white paper generously with water. Add puddles of tempera paint to the wet surface. Let different colors run together. Respray dry areas and add plastic wrap to the wet surface. The wrap will wrinkle as it clings to the wet paint creating interesting channels in the paint. Let dry.

Tip
Planet paper dries more quickly if it is turned plastic side down to dry.

3. Trace and cut circles.

Remove plastic from surface of dry paper and look for interesting places to trace and cut out circles using a circle template or other round object. Save the leftover scraps for landforms.

5. Use scraps to make landforms.

From the leftover scraps, cut unusual or "fantasy" landforms (e.g. valleys, ridges, pinnacles, plateaus). Glue overlapping pieces to the bottom of the black "star" paper. Trim extending pieces even with the black paper.

4. Add black oil pastel to the circles.

To achieve a three-dimensional look, shade each circle with a black oil pastel by coloring a narrow solid black crescent moon on the edge of half of the circle, then blending or smearing this black area inward using a circular motion to create a gradation of dark to light.

6. Add cracks to landforms.

Draw a heavy black oil pastel line along the edge of a torn piece of paper and smear away from this edge while holding the torn paper in place. Remove torn paper to find a crisp edge that looks like a crack or crevice and a smeared area that looks like a cast shadow. Add several more cracks in the same way.

astronomy: the study of objects and matter outside the earth's atmosphere and of their physical and chemical properties.

fantasy space art: art that combines science and our knowledge of the universe to portray imaginary planets and galaxies, landscapes, cities, and civilizations

7. Arrange planets in the sky.

Planets may overlap, sink below the horizon, or float halfway out of the picture. Make sure that shadows are all going in the same direction before gluing down.

8. Add comet tails with chalk.

Choose a few specks in the sky and add comet tails to them by drawing away from the speck in a quick sweeping motion with a piece of white chalk.

9. Draw "beams" of light around a star.

Choose another speck and turn it into an extra bright or "exploding" star by laying a ruler across the center of the speck and drawing six to eight intersecting lines at different angles. The center chalked area can be blended slightly with a fingertip to give it that "glowing" effect.

10. Trace a city dome with chalk.

Place a circle template somewhere in the picture so that it sits about halfway above the horizon. Trace a heavy white chalk line around the inside of this circle. With the template in place, smear this chalk line in toward the center to create a glass dome effect for a city inside.

11. Create a city inside the dome.

Dip an edge of a small square piece of posterboard into a small puddle of white tempera paint and stamp compact vertical lines in varying heights within the dome. Add a few horizontal lines toward the top with an ⅛-in. wide piece of posterboard.

12. Sprinkle glitter on wet city.

While the paint is still wet, sprinkle the fine glitter onto these wet lines.

13. Make pyramids.

Texture a sheet of paper by spattering paint in a variety of colors on it. When dry, snip the corners off and shade ⅓ of the triangles with oil pastel. Place pyramids in the picture and glue in place.

RESOURCES

Art and Everyday Life "Space Art Through the Ages" by Dr. Louis Lankford

Novagraphics – space art, artists, books on space art. Tucson, AZ. 800-727-6682. www.novaspace.com

The Rocket Men: Robert Goddard and Space (video, 60 min.) Goldhil Home Media. www.goldhil.com

Solar System book and CD-ROM. Brooks Cole. www.brookscole.com

STUDENT WORK AGES 11-12

PAUL KLEE LANDSCAPE

CONCEPTS
LANDSCAPE
WATERCOLOR TECHNIQUES:
WET-IN-WET, SALTING,
GLAZING, SPONGING

Paul Klee (1879-1940). *Hilly Country of Porquerolles*, 1927. Pen, 11⅞ x 18⅛ in. ©1982 Dover Publications and its Licensors. © 2005 Artists Rights Society (ARS), NY / VG Bild-Kunst, Bonn

In addition to hundreds of paintings, Swiss-born artist Paul Klee (1879-1940) was also known for his numerous playful line drawings. One piece in particular, *Hilly Country of Porquerolles* created in 1927, is the inspiration for this landscape project. The focus is to capture this expressive Klee line quality in a similar landscape composition. This is accomplished when lines are made by repetitive "stamping" with a piece of mat board dipped in acrylic paint. Added to this foundation of line and structure, is color. Because of their translucent and spontaneous quality, watercolors are used as a contrast to the solid, hard-edged acrylic paint. Four watercolor techniques, wet-on-wet, glazing, sponging, and salt, are incorporated in the process. Like a Klee painting, color is used playfully and unpredictably. Mountains, hills, and valleys are a combination of many blended colors and textures.

MATERIALS
12 x 18-in. bright white construction paper
(sturdy enough for watercolors)
Acrylic paint (dark brown or combination of dark colors – purple, burgundy, black)
Rectangular poster board scraps (⅛ in. to 1½ in.)
Watercolor paints
Paint brush
Salt
Sponges
Water
Aluminum foil

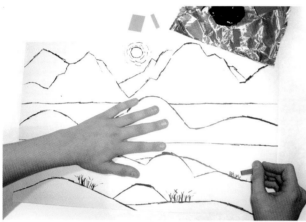

1. Assemble paper, paint, and mat board and begin stamping.

Squeeze a small amount of acrylic paint onto a piece of aluminum foil. Dip the edge of a piece of mat board into the paint and "stamp" horizontal wavy lines across the paper. Lines may weave in and out of each other or disappear and reappear behind other lines. As each line develops, the landscape begins to appear. A landscape project is less intimidating if seen simply as a collection of wavy lines.

Lines toward the bottom appear closest, creating a foreground area in the landscape. Lines in the center create a middleground and the lines closest to the top create the background.

Use a ¼-inch wide piece to stamp tree trunks and branches in the foreground. Bend another piece into a semicircle to stamp a sun or moon in the sky.

Tip

When stamping, discard pieces if they get too saturated and "floppy" with paint.

2. Add watercolor.

Once the acrylic paint is completely dry (a hair dryer can be used), it is safe to add the watercolors.

Note: For the richest colors possible, add a bit of water to each watercolor tray so that paint can soften.

Begin painting using the wet-on-wet technique: wet a selected area of the paper with just water first with a brush, then brush in color and let the colors run on their own within the wetted area. Avoid "scrubbing" different colors together. Choose a new area and repeat the process. Blot away unwanted puddles or muddy areas with a tissue or paper towel.

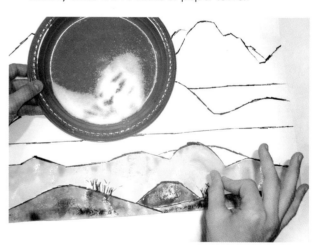

3. Sprinkle grains of salt.

While the paint is shiny wet, sprinkling a few grains of salt into the paint is a nice way to add interesting texture. When the grains touch the wet surface, they begin to dissolve and displace the paint. This creates a little crystal-like back run. The wetter the surface, the larger the crystal shape. Be careful not to overdo the salt or the project will begin to look like sandpaper! The foreground is a logical spot for this technique since this kind of textural detail would not be seen in the distant part of a landscape.

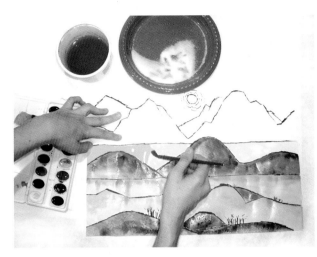

4. Glaze any dry areas that need more intense color.

Since watercolors tend to lighten when they dry, this technique is useful when richer color is desired. It involves adding more watercolor in the same color or analogous color (colors next to each other on the color wheel) on top of an area of color that has dried, such as red over red or yellow over red. If areas are too bright, then glazing with a complementary color, such as yellow over purple, or orange over blue, works to tone down or "quiet" the color as well.

5. Sponge in bushes and rocks.

Torn chunks of sponges are dipped into the moist watercolor paint and stamped at the top of the short vertical lines that were made earlier with the acrylic paint. Sponging in two or three different colors creates depth. Texture can also be sponged into the foreground of the landscape if desired.

landscape: a work of art that uses inland natural scenery as subject matter.

watercolor wet-in-wet: adding a wet watercolor-loaded brush to the wet surface of a paper.

salting: sprinkling grains of salt into wet watercolor to create texture

watercolor glazing: the technique of applying a transparent watercolor wash over a dried color area to achieve luminosity and richness.

sponging: dipping a sponge in watercolor and stamping it on paper to create texture.

STUDENT WORK AGES 10-11

TEXTURES & PATTERNS OF NATURE

CONCEPTS

ELEMENTS: PATTERN, TEXTURE
COLLAGE

Patterns are shapes that are repeated. They are uniform and ordered. Texture is pattern without regularity. It is random and unplanned. These variations, whether subtle or obvious, are what create visual interest in our world around us.

Artists learn to be very aware of these details as they create art. In a two-dimensional work of art, an artist can create the impression of a three-dimensional bumpy or rough surface by carefully observing and employing these variations of repetitive shapes and colors. The impression of texture is purely visual when it cannot be felt. When an artist employs tactile texture, it is texture that can be felt as well as seen. Gluing down bits of colored or textured paper or any other material to a surface, called collage (co-*lahj*), is a means of creating tactile texture.

This project is an exercise in creating both visual and tactile textures: spraying or spattering, stamping, and gluing. Vivid colors heighten the energy and interest.

MATERIALS

Tempera paint (orange, yellow, red, purple, green, brown, magenta – not pictured)

12 x 18-in. yellow construction paper

Soft round paint brush (not pictured)

Posterboard (approx. 2 x 8-in. piece of posterboard, mat board, or other heavy paper)

Watercolors (not pictured) **or spray dyes (Must be used only by an adult)**

Aluminum foil

Colored paper scraps

Oil pastels (set of 12 or 16)

Leaf-shaped sponges (can be purchased as precut shapes at craft stores or made yourself using compressed sponges or from old sponges snipped into simple leaf shapes)

White glue

2. Stamp leaf patterns.

Dispense paint in groups of 2 or 3 colors in any desired combination on pieces of aluminum foil. Let colors run together.

Moisten and squeeze out excess water from sponges, dip into a multicolored puddle of paint and transfer to paper. Press lightly with palm of hand. Repeat. Reload sponge with paint when necessary. Use different leaf shapes.

Tip

Rinse sponges and hands if paint gets too muddy or messy during the process. Wear a smock and roll up your sleeves.

1. Spatter paint on yellow paper.

Place the yellow construction paper in the middle of some newspaper and spatter with two or three different colors of paint by loading a paintbrush with thinned tempera paint and tapping against a pencil held close to the surface or by spraying paint mixed with water from a spray bottle.

pattern: elements repeated over and over, arranged in a predetermined sequence.

texture: the surface quality, both simulated and actual, or artwork.

collage: art technique in which materials such as paper, cloth, or found objects are glued to a backing.

3. Stamp pine needles.

Fold the 2 x 8-in. piece of mat board in half to make two 2 x 4-in. halves. Hold both halves together and bend into a half moon shape. Open halves by inserting a finger inside the fold. Dip into purple paint and stamp the project.

4. Stamp leaves on scraps of paper.

Stamp one or more leaves on a smaller piece of colored paper.

6. Cut out extra leaves and glue into main picture.

Crumple the dry leaves to give them more texture. One or many leaves may be glued.

5. Add veins to leaves.

Once all paint has dried, use oil pastels in various colors to add veins to the inside of each leaf.

STUDENT WORK AGES 9-10

ROCK ART

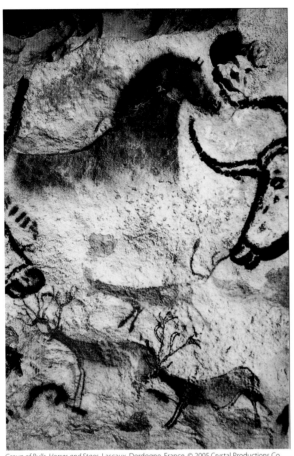

Group of Bulls, Horses and Stags, Lascaux, Dordogne, France. © 2005 Crystal Productions Co. and its Licensors. All Rights Reserved.

TOPICS
CULTURE: NATIVE AMERICAN
    PETROGLYPHS
TECHNIQUES: REPOUSSÉ
    FAUX FINISH
    STAMPING

Engravings and paintings on rock are distributed widely across Europe and North America. Native Americans of many different cultures or tribes, have made Rock Art for thousands of years. Other words for this rock art are pictograph and petroglyph.

Pictographs are images on stone that were created by coloring a rock's surface with powdered minerals, stains from plant substances, or charcoal. In protected areas like caves or under cliffs, these ancient painted images still exist. Petroglyphs are marks or images made on stone by pecking or chipping away some of the stone's surface with another harder rock. They were often made on rocks that were covered with a "rock varnish." Rock varnish is a layer of minerals that becomes attached to a rock's surface. In a dry climate, minerals fly through the air as dust. When dust and water settle on a rock surface, microscopic bacteria on the rock create a surface that causes the minerals to stick and darken over time. When the dark surface is chipped away, it exposes the lighter rock underneath, creating a very bold image that lasts a very long time.

Many of these were sacred sites and probably used for sacred rituals or recording personal spiritual experiences which was very important in Native American cultures. It is difficult to precisely date this rock art but it spans a great period of time.

For this rock art project, the rock varnish will be a mixture of earth-toned enamel spray paints. The chipping-away process is imitated by using a technique of metal embossing called "repoussé" which is explained in the procedure.

MATERIALS

14 x 18-in. piece of Red Rosin paper (thick reddish-brown colored paper used under stucco—available at lumber yards)

6½ x 9-in. piece of 36 gauge aluminum foil (from craft stores or art catalogs)

Enamel spray paints (black, terra cotta, white) **(Must be used only by an adult)**

Ball point pen

Pencil

2-4 sheets 8½ x 11-in. white copy paper

8½ x 11-in. sheet of black card stock

Silver gel pen (optional)

Masking tape

Sand paper (medium or fine)

Glue sticks or clear gel glue (not pictured)

Scissors and/or sheet metal cutters

9 x 12-in. foam with sticky backing (any color)

3 or 4 blocks of wood (1 in. or 1½ in.)

Black ink pad

Native American symbol rubber stamps (optional)

1. Cut Red Rosin paper.

Lay the roll of Red Rosin paper on the floor and measure off 14 inches from the end, fold paper at that point and cut on the crease. Fold this 14 x 36-in. piece in half and cut on the crease again, making two 14 x 18-in. pieces. To flatten each sheet, rub back and forth along the edge of a counter top in the opposite direction of the curl until paper lays flat.

2. Cut aluminum foil.

Unroll the aluminum (it comes 12-in. wide in 5-, 10-, 25-, or 50-ft. rolls at 50 cents a foot) and mark off six inches from the end with a permanent marker. Cut a 6 x 12-in. piece with scissors or metal cutters. Cut this piece down to 6 x 9 inches.

3. Spray aluminum foil with paint.

Center the 6 x 9-in. piece on newspaper and spray with a combination of black and terra cotta spray paints. Set aside to dry.

Tip

Avoid too heavy an application of paint. A heavy, "gummy" layer is more difficult to sand down later.

5. Make a petroglyph drawing.

Lay the dried 6 x 9-in. foil piece on top of an 8½ x 11-in. sheet of white paper and trace around it. Trim off excess so that it fits exactly to the foil. Remove paper from foil and draw a petroglyph design in pencil on the white paper.

Tip

Remind students that this is a drawing of "floating" symbols and not a landscape with a horizon line. Varying the size and placement of shapes will more closely resemble a real petroglyph.

4. Spray Red Rosin paper with paint.

Center the 14 x 18-in. piece of Red Rosin paper on some newspaper and lightly spray "cracks" around the edges with black, terra cotta, and white spray paints using the torn pieces of the 8½ x 11-in. white paper. Turn the torn paper in all directions to create interesting random patterns. Use two or more torn pieces for variations.

6. Trace over drawing on the foil.

Tape the finished drawing in place on top of the painted side of the foil and trace over it with the ball point pen. Putting a layer of newspaper underneath and good pressure on the pen on top will ensure a good design transfer into the foil.

7. Sand the foil.

Once the design has been completely traced, remove the pattern and begin sanding the surface. Sand down to the metal around all of the drawn shapes so that they stand out against the dark paint.

8. Tear the edges off the sheet of black cardstock.

Tear the edge off all four sides of this sheet. Use both hands to control the tear. Center and glue the 6 x 9-in. foil piece into the center of this torn black paper.

petroglyph: a carving or inscription on rock.

repoussé: metal that is shaped or ornamented with patterns in relief made by hammering or pressing on the reverse side.

faux finish: a decorative paint technique that imitates a pattern found in nature, such as marble or wood.

stamping: a technique in which paint or ink is applied to an image or pattern that has been carved onto a soft block and then pressed onto any type of media so that the image is transferred to the media.

9. Add designs around the edge of the paper.

Use the silver gel pen to add additional designs around the edge of the black paper. Center and glue this to the 14 x 18-in. piece of Red Rosin paper.

10. Stamp the paper with Native American symbols.

Finally, add a few interesting shapes to the border area using purchased rubber stamps and a stamp pad or your own stamps made from wood blocks, a foam sheet with sticky backing, and scissors. Simply draw a shape, cut and peel away backing, and stick it to the block and begin stamping. Add ink to stamp pad for best results. (See rock art symbols on following page.)

REPTILE RELIEF

Wassily Kandinsky (1866-1944), *White Zig-zags*. 1922. Galleria d'Arte Moderna di Ca' Pesaro, Venice, Italy. Photo Credit : Cameraphoto Arte, Venice / Art Resource, NY. © 2005 Artists Rights Society (ARS), NY / ADAGP, Paris

CONCEPTS
ABSTRACT ART
NONOBJECTIVE ART
RELIEF

Abstract art evolved in the beginning of the 20th century after photography proved its ability to capture the world as it was. Abstract artists sought to convey what could not be seen through a camera lens. What they tried to convey were the essential characteristics of an object with a stylized or symbolic reflection of its reality.

Wassily Kandinsky is considered to be the first artist to have achieved a truly abstract visual language in painting. His earliest works during 1910 contained some connection to the real world (abstract), but later his art abandoned all reference to recognizable form and emerged as a style called "nonobjective." The intention of this nonobjective style is for the viewer to simply respond to the lines, shapes, and colors themselves without any reference to recognizable objects.

By superimposing these two styles in a relief, this project helps to solidify an understanding of the differences. Relief is a term used when part of the surface is raised. In this case, it is an abstract style reptile against a nonobjective background of painted lines and chalk pastels.

MATERIALS
Two 12 x18-in. sheets of black construction paper
White tempera paint
Soft round paint brush (not pictured)
Colored Chalk
Scissors
Glue stick or clear gel glue (not pictured)
Pencil
Foam board (Cut into small bits)
Reptile patterns (See page 32)

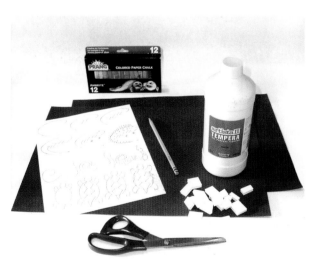

1. Paint black paper with a network of connecting white lines.

These lines may be bold, delicate, curved, or straight. Add a second coat for a solid white appearance.

2. Color black areas with chalk.

When lines connect, shapes are created. In this case, all the black areas between the lines are the shapes. Fill these in with chalk in solid, mixed, or blended colors. Avoid blowing chalk dust off the project. Instead, using fingers, blend the loose chalk into the project. Any excess after that can be "tapped" off by holding paper on its side and tapping on the table.

nonobjective: art which has no recognizable subject matter, such as trees, flowers, or people. The real subject matter is the composition of the drawing or painting itself.

abstract: a style of art that shows objects, people, and/or places in simplified arrangements of shape, line, texture, and color, often geometrical.

relief: the raised parts of a surface which are often noticeable by the feeling of texture.

3. Draw a reptile.

On the separate piece of black paper, draw a reptile (snake, lizard, turtle, alligator, etc.) Steps here include a snake, turtle, and Iguana. See templates on page 32. The drawings are purposely simplified/stylized to imitate the abstract style and to make painting and cutting easier later on.

Tip

To avoid having blended colors become too muddy looking, clean fingers with a wet paper towel or rag periodically.

5. Cut out reptile and add styrofoam.

Once dry, cut out reptile and glue enough styrofoam bits on the back so that it will pop up evenly. Be sure that the styrofoam bits cannot be seen from the front.

4. Paint and color the reptile drawing.

Paint over the pencil lines of the finished reptile drawing with white paint. When dry, add chalk to fill in the black areas, then paint a second coat of white paint if necessary.

6. Attach reptile to nonobjective art.

Place the reptile so that it extends beyond the paper as if it were crawling into or out of the picture. Experiment with different solutions before attaching with rubber cement.

STUDENT WORK AGES 9-10

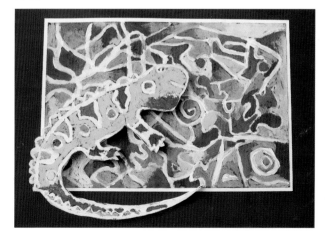

AFRICAN MASK

African Mask. © 2005 Corbis

TOPIC
AFRICAN CUSTOMS
CONCEPT
ABSTRACT COLLAGE

Africa's traditional arts, like its beliefs, are concerned mainly with spiritual content. Masks are created to be dwelling places for spirits. African masks represent Gods, ancestors of great wisdom, or monsters familiar in the myths and beliefs of each tribe. The mask is sought as a medium to transform the wearer into another being who possesses supernatural abilities. Masks express and celebrate the moral and religious convictions that underlay daily life. They are created to be worn in tribal religious ceremonies and ritualistic dances and are a way of connecting with the supernatural world for various reasons: initiation rites, ensure health or fertility, teach laws and traditions, administer justice, influence forces of nature, embody spirit of deceased, mark territories. Mask makers practice intense meditation and concentration when creating a mask often secluding themselves to keep the mask concealed during its creation. Rules for how a mask must look and how it is made are handed down from generation to generation. Their mysterious, sometimes tortured, and often terrifying lines express the ultimate in supernatural forces.

Picasso admired and used the African mask style to help develop the newly emerging abstract art in Europe which, like African art, sought to convey what the artist knew or felt about his subject matter.

Most African masks are made from green wood that is blackened in a fire. Other materials are added such as beeswax, jute, feathers, seeds, shells, clay, and metal. For exciting color and texture, this project uses of a variety of materials and incorporates Adinkra symbols and African motifs.

MATERIALS
12 x 18-in. bright white construction paper
Pencil
Scissors
Dried beans (black, pinto, etc.)
Raffia (natural and/or black paper twist)
Synthetic animal fur pieces (black or brown)
Spray dyes (Must be used only by an adult)
Tissue paper (assorted colors)
Liquid starch
Paint brush
Oil pastels
Permanent markers and/or watercolor markers
Watercolors
African stamps (instructions on page 36)
White glue

1. Draw a mask.

On the 12 x 18-in. construction paper, draw an African mask in pencil then cover the pencil lines with a black permanent marker. Refer to mask templates on page 37 for ideas.

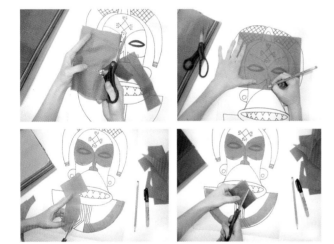

2. Cut pieces of tissue paper for the mask drawing.

Choose areas for tissue paper. Lay a piece over the drawing and trace and cut out the shape.

abstract collage: a work of art which utilizes simplified or symbolic forms and materials such as paper, cloth, or found objects that are glued to a backing. Subject matter may be recognizable or may be completely transformed into shapes, colors, and/or lines.

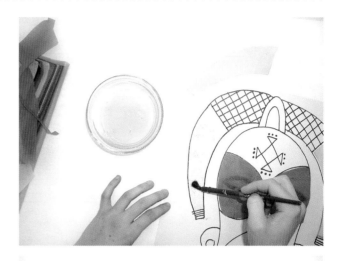

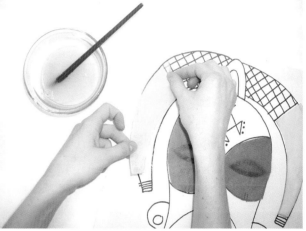

3. Glue tissue to mask.

Brush the liquid starch onto the mask and adhere the tissue. Brush over the top.

4. Color areas of mask with marker.

Permanent markers will not bleed when sprayed with dye which is done in step 5.

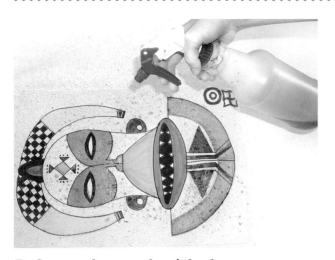
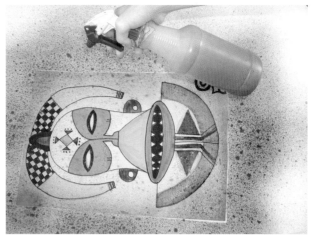

5. Spray the mask with dye.

Begin with yellow. Add red, then blue. Blue will turn green on the yellow. Choose areas for each color. If colors overlap too much, the results will be dull and muddy. Let this dry.

6. Untwist black raffia and snip into "fringe."

This raffia often goes by the name of "paper twist." Cut off lengths of this rope, untwist, snip, and glue onto mask.

7. Glue black beans and fur pieces to mask.

Use the white glue for both.

8. Make African stamps.

Inexpensive pine boards 1-in. x 2-in. x 4-ft. can be cut into small squares and rectangles at a lumber yard or at home with an electric miter saw. Use the wood pieces to trace the shapes on the sticky-backed foam sheets. Cut these out and draw designs on the front. Cut designs out and adhere to wood blocks. Refresh ink pads with refill ink if necessary for nice dark images or ink the stamp directly with the refill bottle.

STUDENT WORK AGES 9-10

THE BLAZING BANYAN TREE

Banyan Tree. © Thinkstock

CONCEPTS

NEGATIVE SPACE
BLENDING
REFLECTIONS

There is an unusual and amazing tree that originates in India called the "banyan tree." It is unusual because it has so many trunks. The branches of this massive tree are constantly sending out roots from the top that anchor into the soil below and expand to become additional trunks. A single banyan tree may cover an area nearly 1,500 feet in circumference and have more than 3,000 trunk-like roots. If a bird or other animal were to deposit a banyan seed on another tree, the seedling would send its tentacles down to earth and eventually create a network of roots that would engulf and destroy the host tree. The banyan is sacred to the Hindus. They give it its name, which means "trader," because markets are held under its vast sheltering framework.

This interesting tree from the mulberry family is the subject for this project which introduces the concept of "negative space." The interesting pockets of space that are created within the branches and trunks of this drawing are the "negative space" (or space around the object). Compositions are improved when artists give careful attention to the space around objects and how they relate to the subject in a painting rather than leaving this space empty. This project uses "blazing" color (blended oil pastels) to anchor the tree into the picture.

The tree may also be made to appear to be sitting in a pool of water if reflections are added.

MATERIALS

White drawing paper (12 x 18 in. or smaller)
Pencil
Black liquid tempera paint
Soft medium round paint brush
Oil pastels (all colors–set of 12 or 16)

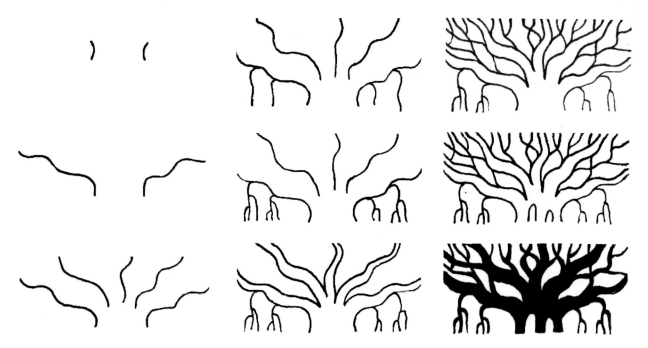

1. Draw banyan tree.

Lay paper horizontally and begin by drawing two opposite curving lines about 4 inches apart and about 4 inches from the bottom of the paper. Add two wavy lines that connect to these first two lines and extend diagonally in opposite directions to the edge of the paper.

Add three more evenly spaced wavy lines between these first two lines.

negative space: area around objects in a work of art; in a two-dimensional work of art, sometimes called the background.

blending: combining or mixing colors in a work of art to create a smooth transition between colors.

reflection: transformation which produces the mirror image of an object.

Tip

Students are not restricted to a banyan tree. Any tree will utilize these drawing concepts (e.g., going from large to small, extending to the edge of the paper, overlapping).

Add lines that curve down from the bottom branches and also stop 4 inches from the bottom of the paper. Add more that subdivide from these. Give the tree mass by drawing parallel lines next to those already drawn. Begin wide at the base and taper at the tips.

Add smaller branches that overlap and connect to larger branches or extend to the edge of the paper.

Add two or three "tunnels" in the base of the trunk.

2. Paint the banyan tree.

Paint this pencil drawing with black tempera paint using a medium or fine brush. Work away from the freshly painted areas to avoid smearing the paint.

3. Color background with oil pastels.

When the paint has dried, add oil pastels to white areas. Use fingers to blend colors. The vibrant, velvety look comes from heavy application and blending of the oil pastels. Clean fingers periodically with a paper towel.

4. Create water reflections.

Use black oil pastel to add irregular zig zag lines where the tree trunks meet the water in order to create the appearance of reflections on the water.

Tip

When all areas have been filled in with color, go back and touch up tree parts with black oil pastel.

STUDENT WORK AGES 11-12

CERAMIC CASTLE

Castelnaud Castle, SW France.
Photo © 2005 Crystal Productions

TOPIC
MEDIEVAL CASTLES
CONCEPTS
CLAY
CLAY TECHNIQUES: SLAB METHOD, EMBOSS, INCISE

Castles were fortified homes that began in medieval Europe. In the fifth century, the Roman Empire collapsed. It was split into many kingdoms and by the 10th century, 900 to 1300, feudalism, a decentralized form of government prevailed. During this time, no kings and not even the Holy Roman Emperor had any real control over all the areas he claimed. It was up to the individual feudal lords to see to their own protection. As a result, castles began to appear in the 1100s to serve as a fortress as well as a residence to protect their owner and his family, land, servants and private army of knights. In spite of the romanticized fairy tales, a medieval castle was actually a dark, damp, and drafty place to live. Windows were small and walls became as thick as 30 feet in order to withstand invaders with catapults, battering rams, and artillery. Priority was given to protection not comfort. It wasn't until the 1600s that improved cannons that could break through the thickest walls doomed castles as a fortress. As governmental power became more centralized again and times more peaceful, castles became a place of royal residence with priority to embellishment and comfort.

Most medieval castles had a similar layout. Inside the outer walls, among other things, was a tower or "keep" where the lord of the castle resided and which served as a final stronghold in case all other defenses failed. This project is a version of this structure and includes an ascending stairway, windows, parapet, and pennant flags.

Notes about clay:

Clay is a pliable mixture of earth and water. It can be found naturally in pockets in the earth but most often it is created using a recipe. The most abundant components in clay are silica, alumina, and water but there can be many other mineral contents. The microscopic particles are much smaller and flatter than regular soil. The plate-like particles that cling closely together and slip around easily in the water content, are what make it much more cohesive and pliable than regular soil.

Children love to work with clay. With a minimal search, you can locate an art supply store that carries the "low fire" ceramic clay used in this project and a location where it can be fired in a kiln. "Low fire" clay indicates the temperature to which it is fired, usually cone 06 or 1,873 degrees. The cost of clay is about 6-9 dollars for 25 pounds. Each castle uses about 2 pounds.

MATERIALS

Low fire (06) ceramic clay (sand or "grog" added is preferable but not necessary)

Clay roller (this could be a wood rolling pin or a wood dowel that is about 1¼ inch in diameter and 18 inches long)

2 wood slats (about ⅜ x 1⅛ x 18 inches)

Clay cutting tool (or butter knife)

Castle pattern (shown on next page)

1-in. PVC pipe (cut 7½ inches long)

Newspaper

Fishing line (or heavy string, wire, or dental floss)

Glue sticks or clear gel glue (not pictured)

2 bamboo skewers

White art paper (small piece or scrap)

Fluorescent spray paint (Pink, yellow, or blue)

(Must be used only by an adult)

Tip

Sand or grog (ground up bisque ware) is often added to clay to reduce shrinkage, cracking, and sagging.

1. Cut a slab of clay.

Open a 25 lb. block of clay, lay it on its side lengthwise, and using both hands, cut off a slab by pulling a taut fishing line evenly through the clay about ¾-in. deep.

2. Roll out clay slab.

Lay the slab of clay in the center of some heavy paper or cloth, arrange sticks lengthwise on either side but not touching the clay. Roll the clay out until the thickness is uniform with the sticks.

Note: When rolling, avoid beginning right in the center. Instead, roll out small perimeter sections and work progressively toward the center. Lift and reposition the clay if necessary, but to maintain a consistent thickness, the sticks must be in place so that the rolling pin always has contact with them.

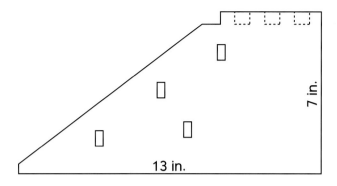

7 in.

13 in.

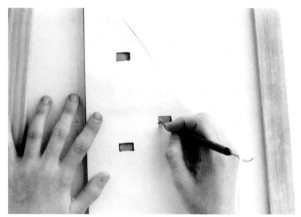

3. Cut out pattern.

Lay the paper pattern over the slab and check for fit. If the clay is short anywhere, then cut away excess clay from another area and over lap the two pieces in the needed spot and roll out again. Keep scraps moist in a plastic bag.

4. Cut out windows.

Use the clay tool to incise windows where indicated in the pattern. Remove the excess clay from window by lifting the slab and pushing clay out through the back with the clay tool or a finger.

5. Add a stairway.

Push a block of wood into the clay along the diagonal side in an even interval keeping the block at right angles to the bottom.

6. Stamp brick patterns.

With a smaller block of wood (about ¼ x ½ in.) stamp brick patterns everywhere. The pattern should be random to merely "suggest" a brick construction. Always stamp either vertically or horizontally.

9. Roll clay castle around the pipe.

Turn the slab of clay brick side facing down and roll around the newspaper covered pipe beginning from the wide end.

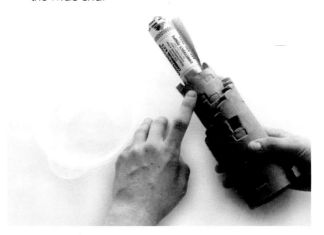

7. Make a parapet.

Cut out sections of clay in the top of the tower to create a parapet or raised and recessed edge. This design was intended to protect soldiers in battle.

10. Repair unwanted cracks.

Cracks can be smoothed out with water on a fingertip or left intentionally. Windows may also be cut all the way through to the pipe at this time with the clay tool.

clay: a mud-like sediment composed of very fine particles of minerals. Pliable when moist, but becomes hard when dry or fired.

incise: to engrave or carve into a surface.

slab method: refers to a ceramic process in which the artist assembles an artwork by hand using flat slabs of clay that have been rolled to a consistent thickness.

8. Roll newspaper around PVC pipe.

Make the newspaper 1 or 2 inches higher than the pipe and secure with a bit of tape. The newspaper will prevent the clay from sticking to the pipe.

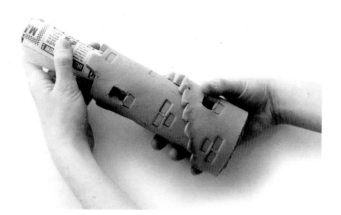

11. Remove PVC pipe.

If the clay is not too moist, you can almost immediately remove the pipe by pushing up from the bottom and pulling from the top. The newspaper will allow it to slide free. Do not leave the pipe inside for very long or it will crack the project since clay shrinks as it dries. Let the castle air dry completely (2-6 days depending on humidity). Be sure and correct any flaws before clay hardens (e.g., sagging or cracked windows, stairs, or parapet).

13. Paint the castle.

The castle in this project does not require a glaze firing. It is painted with watercolors and spray paint. Watercolors work well because the color is absorbed into the clay to create soft variations that combine well with the translucent spray paints that are added next. Paint the top inside portion of the castle as well. Check all sides for coverage. Since the surface is so absorbent, it will be necessary to add water frequently to the paints.

14. Spray paint the castle.

Once the castle has been painted with watercolors, random touches of spray paint, in flourescent pink, yellow, blue or green will intensify color variations and add to the whimsical aspect of the project. Protect your hand from the spray paint with a plastic bag if you are holding the castle while spraying hard to reach areas.

12. Fire castle in a kiln.

This completely dry piece of "green ware" is now ready for the kiln. It will go through a "bisque firing." Low fire clay can be bisque fired at either cone 06 or 03 (1,873-2,068 degrees).

Tip

Many ceramic shops will fire your work for a small fee. A medium size kiln will generally hold projects for a class of 25-30 in a single firing.

15. Add glitter to the castle.

Apply glue with a glue stick, then sprinkle the fine iridescent glitter sparingly over the entire castle.

Extra information on firing clay:

A "cone" is an inch long cone or bar of clay (also called pyrometric bar) placed in the kiln to melt at a precise temperature to indicate when the kiln should be turned off or to trip a mechanism that automatically shuts the kiln off. Depending on the number of pieces in the kiln, this temperature will be reached in 3 to 9 hours and require approximately another 9 hours to cool down. The fired piece is considered ceramic and will not dissolve in water as green ware does. It must go through a second firing if it is glazed.

16. Add flags to castle.

The two bamboo skewers are attached to flags then spray painted and/or colored with markers. To make the flags, fold the sheet of white art paper in half and cut out two wavy pennant flag shapes. Each flag shape can be opened like a book, glued on the inside and wrapped around the top of each skewer.

Lay the flags flat and color or spray both sides of the flags and sticks with paint. If desired, add glitter as well. Place the flagpoles inside the castle. Adjust the height by cutting excess length off the bottom of the sticks with scissors but keep them long enough so that they touch the bottom. Glue with a thick sticky glue. Hold flags in place with tape until the glue dries. Bend the flags to appear as if they are waving in the breeze.

RESOURCES

Medieval Castles by Conrad Cairns (Minneapolis: Lerner Pub. 1989)

Castles of the Middle Ages by Pierre Miquel (Massachusetts: Silver, Burdett & Ginn Pub., 1985)

PRINTMAKING/ PAPER WEAVING

CONCEPTS

PRINTMAKING
ORGANIC LINE

Printmaking is a unique process in which a raised or recessed image is created on a flat surface of wood, metal, or plastic then transferred or duplicated onto another surface, usually paper, by adding either ink, watercolor, oil paint or water soluble colored pencils to the surface of the image, then paper and pressure. The transfer can be made either by hand (rubbing the paper with your hand or a smooth rubbing tool) or with a printing press. The image can be re-inked and used many times. If the image or "plate" is painted differently each time, each print will be unique; otherwise a sturdy plate can produce hundreds of near identical pieces of art called an "edition."

The earliest prints were made by the Italian printmaker Giovanni Benedetto Castlione and Dutch artist Rembrandt van Rijn around 1645. Giovanni used the "subtractive" technique. He rolled ink onto a metal plate and wiped away places to make an image. Rembrandt used a metal tool to scratch lines into the metal plate then wiped away everything except the ink trapped in the lines.

This project incorporates a styrofoam sheet and a ballpoint pen to create a printing plate. This is a familiar idea but if the styrofoam surface is lightly sanded with sandpaper, the plate will "accept" watercolors quite nicely instead of the standard printing inks. The result is completely different. Watercolors achieve many subtle color variations in the image as well as interesting "backruns" (where denser puddles of pigment collect and create edges) whereas printing inks aim to produce consistently even and uniform prints. By using watercolor, each print is unique and because of its unpredictability, every print is a new discovery. The subject matter for the design is nonobjective, organic lines or lines that are "free-flowing" — without sharp corners or uniform pattern and without reference to any recognizable object. Styrofoam sheets in various sizes for printmaking can be purchased through art catalogs; however, the center out of a large styrofoam dinner plate or lid off of a styrofoam container also works. This project uses a 6 x 6-in. piece. Keeping it square eliminates any confusion during the weaving process. The prints are dried then examined closely for interesting "edges" (backruns and white lines left from the recessed lines on the plate) to be outlined in ink. Two prints are then woven together, enhanced with metal pieces and a unique frame you create yourself.

printmaking: the art of making works of art from one of the four printmaking processes (relief, intaglio, lithography, and serigraphy). Characterized by multiple impressions of a single image. Not to be confused with a machine-made print of a work of art or "art reproduction."

organic lines: lines that are free-form, or having a quality that resembles living things. The opposite of mechanical or geometric.

1. Cut Styrofoam plate.

Cut a 6 x 6-in. piece from a large Styrofoam plate and sand lightly with a piece of sandpaper. Mark the plate with a square and cut with a mat knife. Use medium coarse (#220) sandpaper and rub lightly over entire surface of the square.

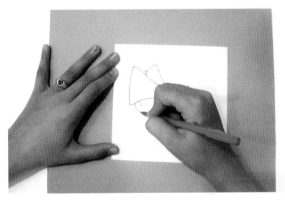

2. Draw image on Styrofoam.

Use enough pressure on the ball point pen so that it will indent the surface without tearing through. Create a drawing that has soft, curving, irregular lines and shapes (organic) without reference to subject matter (nonobjective).

3. Paint Styrofoam with watercolors.

Paint the entire surface with a mixture of colors using enough water to make it shiny wet. If any paint has spilled beyond the plate, then move the plate to a clean surface before making a print. After the first print, sand any areas that still repel paint.

MATERIALS

Square Styrofoam sheet (about 6 x 6 inches)

Ballpoint pen

Paper (medium weight, absorbent)

Paper towel (or clean rag)

Watercolor paints

Paint brush

Fine tip permanent black marker

Mat knife (also called a utility knife or hobby knife)
(Must be used only by an adult)

Mat board (small piece, about 10 x 10 inches, for a cutting surface)

Glue sticks or clear gel glue (not pictured)

Sand paper (about #220 coarseness)

Paper for frame (could be crumpled paper sack, construction paper, or any purchased handmade papers)

Metallic paint pen (gold, silver, or copper)

Metallic spray paint (gold, silver, or copper)
(Must be used only by an adult)

Purple tempera paint

Water buckets

Latex gloves (or rubber gloves)

4. Make a print.

Carefully center a piece of paper on top of this painted plate and rub the back completely with a cloth or paper towel until you can see that the entire image has been absorbed into the paper. Carefully peel away the sheet and dry. Repeat this process to make 3 or 4 prints. Experiment with different colors.

Tip

It is a good idea to move the plate away from the painting area to make the prints so no unwanted color is transferred to the prints.

5. Add fine black lines.

Choose the best two prints and outline the edges caused by backruns in the paint or by the recessed print pattern with a fine tip black permanent marker. The amount of outlining is an individual preference.

6. Cut slits into a print.

Place a print on the piece of mat board and cut slits with the mat knife that are about ½-in. apart going just to the edge of the print. It does not matter if the slits are cut from top to bottom or side to side.

7. Cut another print into strips.

Cut another print into ½-in. strips that are still connected slightly at one end. Tear or cut each strip off one at a time as they are needed and weave into the first print. Don't weave strips out of order or they will not fit as snugly.

8. Cut the last strip into ten squares.

Arrange five pieces at either end of the weaving in various positions and glue into place.

9. Insert additional strips of paper or metal into the weaving.

Cut white paper into small, narrow strips (about ⅛ x 1½ inches) and insert them randomly into the weaving. Bits of aluminum or copper foil or paper strips sprayed with metallic paint work as well.

10. Make a paper sack frame.

Soak paper sacks in water and open seams, wad into a ball, and submerge in a bucket of water and ⅛ cup purple tempera paint (just enough to cover the sacks). Let paper sit in the mixture for a minute then carefully squeeze and remove. Paint will be darkest in the creases. Lay flat to dry. Press the dry piece with an iron and cut into a frame 7 x 8½ inches on the inside and 12 x 14 inches on the outside. Add highlights to the wrinkles with a metallic pen. Center the weaving inside the frame and tape and/or glue together.

Tip

A frame could also be made from construction paper treated with metallic spray paint or from an attractive handmade paper.

SEASHORE TREASURES

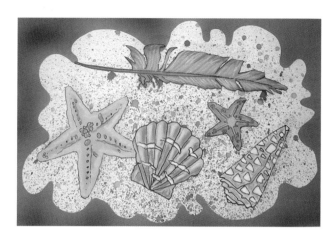

Tip

Encourage students to make shell drawings that fill each sheet of paper to discourage just tracing around the shells.

contour drawing: a single line drawing which defines the outer and inner forms (contours) of people or objects.

balance: a principle of design that refers to the equalization of elements in a work of art. There are three kinds of balance: symmetrical, asymmetrical, and radial.

movement: a principle of design that refers to the arrangement of parts in a drawing to create a slow to fast flow of your eye through the work.

CONCEPTS
CONTOUR DRAWING
PRINCIPLES: BALANCE, MOVEMENT

A contour drawing is a line drawing that describes the edges of forms or shapes. It requires close attention to details so that it becomes a careful, precise, and accurate description of the object. Contour drawing improves concentration (focus), eye-hand coordination (ability to draw what you see), and the ability to observe details and to make a relationship between one part of the drawing to another part (proportion). Artists often do contour drawing to develop and practice their skills. If children are exposed to this approach, it can help them start to break away from relying on drawing the symbols they have learned to represent their world and more closely observe their environment. Small interesting objects like shells offer the opportunity to observe a three-dimensional object more carefully. Because each child can actually handle the shells they draw, they are more likely to look at them frequently and include details as they draw. It is good to describe the lines not in terms of the object (e.g., the bottom of the shell) but rather the characteristics of the line itself (e.g., a curving bumpy line). The asymmetry of the shells makes them less intimidating to draw. If one side of a drawing does not match the other side, it still looks good because shells are not exactly the same on both sides. It is expected that many initial drawings will lack sensitivity and accuracy; however, it is good to acknowledge and point out the parts of their drawings that capture a unique character of a particular shell. To stimulate their interest, this lesson uses the contour drawing itself as only one component of a larger, more colorful composition. These drawings incorporate colorful paper, chalk, and spray dyes. The principles of balance and movement come into play when the shells are positioned and glued on the "sand." A balanced piece will have equal interest in all areas and movement that keeps the viewer's eye moving within the picture. In relief, the shells cast shadows that also become an element of design in the picture.

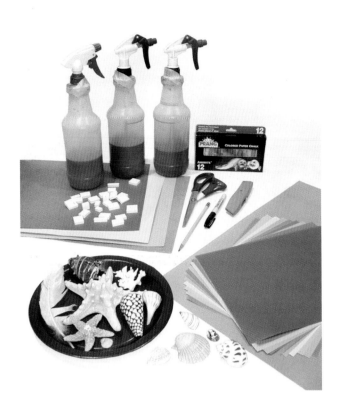

1. Spray texture on 12 x 18-in. white paper.

Center the paper on newspaper and lightly spray red, blue, and yellow paint or dye on the surface. Set aside to dry.

MATERIALS

12 x 18-in. construction paper (yellow, blue, purple, red or orange)

8½ x 11-in. colored copy paper (bright yellow, pink, orange, green, blue, purple, turquoise, lime green, light red)

Pencil

Colored chalk

Scissors

Fine tip permanent black marker

Spray paint (dye or tempera paint and water in a spray bottle) (**Must be used only by an adult**)

Glue sticks or clear gel glue (not pictured)

Sea shells

Foam board

Mat board

Mat knife (Must be used only by an adult)

2. Assemble shells, paper, pencil, marker, and chalk and begin to draw.

Choose at least three shells and make contour drawings of each shell on three different colored sheets of the copy paper. Make the drawings larger than the actual shells.

3. Outline the pencil drawings with a fine tip black marker.

4. Add chalk to areas in each shell drawing.

If desired, blend the chalk to look soft and subtle. Let the paper show through.

5. Cut out shell shapes.

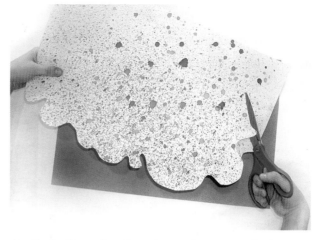

6. Cut the dry textured paper into a wavy shape.

Cut out a free-hand shape or draw a wavy line completely around the edges of the sheet (on the back) and cut along the pencil line.

7. Glue the textured shape to construction paper.

Place the wavy shape on newspaper, apply glue, and attach to a sheet of 12 x 18-in. construction paper in a color that enhances the artwork.

Tip

If you do not live near the shore, many arts and crafts stores sell packages of shells. You could also substitute found objects such as pinecones, sticks, and leaves, or use small vegetables for this project.

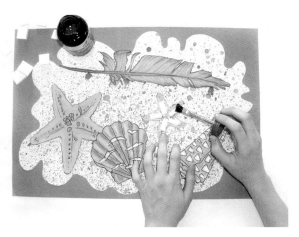

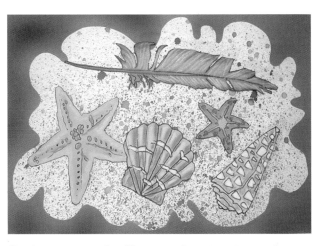

8. Add foam bits to the back of each shell.

Use glue to attach foam bits. Make sure they cannot be seen from the front.

9. Arrange shells on the textured surface and glue down.

Create a pleasing, balanced arrangement of the shells before gluing into place.

STUDENT WORK AGES 11-12

REPOUSSÉ REPTILES

TOPIC
MEXICAN CULTURE
CONCEPTS
FOLK ART
REPOUSSÉ

Crafts in Mexico are an essential part of life. Regions are defined and supported by their crafts, considered folk art. The skills are handed down as family tradition. It is also a cultural heritage that links to the past.

In ancient Mexico, images were sculptured in relief, or embossed into sheets of metal, most often gold. Today images from the past are incorporated into a more economical metal, tin. Sheets of tin are embossed and trimmed into whimsical creatures – armadillos, exotic birds, tropical fish, Mayan gods, roosters, skeletons, angels, churches, and of course, reptiles. They are then colored with brightly colored lacquer paints.

This project imitates this folk art with aluminum foil, bright fluorescent permanent markers, and whimsical reptile shapes. The process of embossing images into sheet metal is called repoussé (ruh-poo-*say*). It dates back to 1600 B.C. Greece. In this project, three-dimensional shapes are created with foam board and and covered with foil and then the aluminum foil is embossed with underlying raised designs.

MATERIALS
Butcher paper (or two 8½ x 14-in. sheets of paper)
Foam board (20 x 30-in. sheet)
Pencil
Scissors
Mat knife (Must be used only by an adult)
Mat board (cutting surface)
Styrofoam plate
Aluminum foil (not pictured)
Glue sticks or clear gel glue (not pictured)
Permanent markers (in bright colors)
Masking tape
Tissue lamé (thin, metallic looking fabric)
Aluminum flashing (building material)
Metal cutters (Must be used only by an adult)

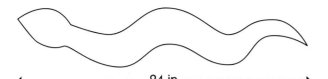

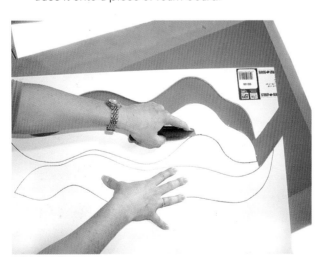

1. Draw, cut, and trace a reptile pattern.

Butcher paper or two 8½ x 14-in. sheets taped end to end provide the size paper needed for this 24-in. long reptile pattern. The drawing simply involves making two parallel wavy lines that converge at either end. The widest part is about 3 inches wide and one end has one last bulge for a head. Cut this out and trace it onto a piece of foam board.

2. Cut out reptile shape.

Place a mat board piece underneath the foam board and cut out the reptile shape with a mat knife. Put a fresh blade into the knife for a nice clean cut. Dull blades tend to shred the Styrofoam. (Cardboard could be substituted.)

3. Cut out geometric shapes and glue to the reptile.

Pieces can be cut from a Styrofoam plate or scraps of mat board with scissors. Cut them to fit the reptile and include things like squares, triangles, rectangles, circles, zigzags, diamonds. Use glue to attach pieces. Create repeating patterns or random designs.

4. Glue reptile to foil.

Apply glue to the reptile shape and attach aluminum foil by placing the reptile face down on the dull side of a piece of foil. Two snakes will fit side by side on one length of foil.

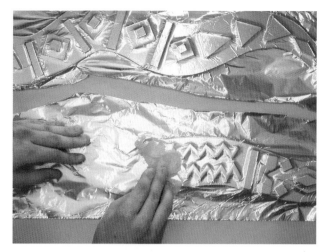

5. Smooth, trim and wrap the foil.

Trim away excess foil leaving enough extra foil to wrap around to the back. Tape down any places that pop up in the back then turn the reptile over and rub with a cloth to smooth and emboss the foil with the raised pattern that is underneath.

6. Color foil with markers.

Start with the lightest colors first to avoid contaminating them with the darker colors. Add line details with a fine black marker, if desired, at the end of the process.

7. Decorate the snake with sequins.

Glue sequins to the snake to add eyes, nostrils, and decoration to the body of the snake.

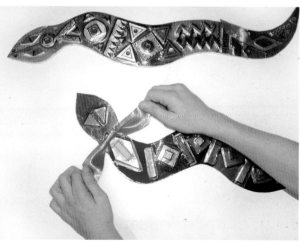

8. Add a neckerchief to the snake.

Cut a piece of tissue lamé fabric on the bias (diagonal) about 14 inches long by 1½ inches wide and tie into a square knot around the neck. Trim away the excess length.

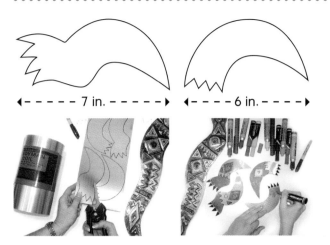

9. Make arms and legs for the lizard.

If you are making a lizard, enlarge the patterns above to make arms and legs. Cut the pattern out and trace onto the aluminum flashing. Be sure to reverse each pattern when tracing the second leg. Cut these out with metal cutters and color them with permanent markers. Bend each piece into an arch and insert into the sides of the body. This step is best done by an adult. If the sharp tips do not go straight into the Styrofoam, they can break through the surface. Add tape on the back, if needed, to secure the legs.

folk art: handicrafts and ornamental works produced by people with no formal art training but trained in traditional techniques often handed down through generations and of a specific region.

repoussé: metal hammered into a relief design from the back. Also called embossing.

STUDENT WORK

RADIAL SYMMETRY IN DESIGN

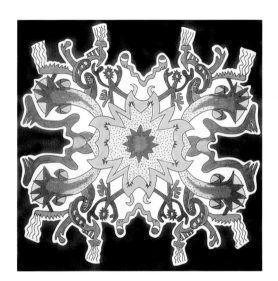

CONCEPTS

RADIAL SYMMETRY
A/B PATTERN
ORGANIC/GEOMETRIC

Radial symmetry refers to designs that have a clearly defined axis of symmetry or where repeating patterns converge to a center point. Radial symmetry creates a strong center of interest and is a way of organizing many elements. It is often used in architecture to unify and strengthen complex designs such as found in the dome of our U.S. capitol building; the intricate stained glass windows of Europe's cathedrals; in a pattern woven into a reed basket; in the Japanese art form Kirigami; in Islamic Arabesque designs; in nature – flowers, snowflakes, spider webs; and the list goes on.

This project incorporates an A/B pattern process around a center point to transform original drawings into beautiful complex-radial designs. The subject matter centers around organic or free-flowing lines that range from realistic to stylized plant forms.

MATERIALS

12 x 12-in. white sulfite drawing paper (or any sturdy paper that is translucent enough to trace through)

6 x 6-in. white sulfite drawing paper

Pencil

Fine tip black permanent marker

Watercolor markers, colored pencils, or watercolor paints

Black construction paper

Scissors

Glue sticks or clear gel glue (not pictured)

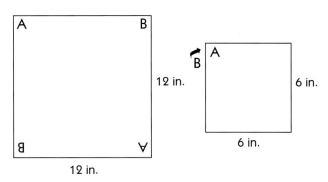

1. Mark the sheets of paper with A/B.

With a pencil, mark the upper left corner of the 12 x 12-in. sheet with an "A" and the upper right corner with a "B." Turn the paper 180 degrees and mark the two new corners at the top in the same way.

On the 6 x 6-in. sheet, put an "A" in the upper left corner (the same as the larger sheet); however, put a "B" right behind the "A" on the back of the paper.

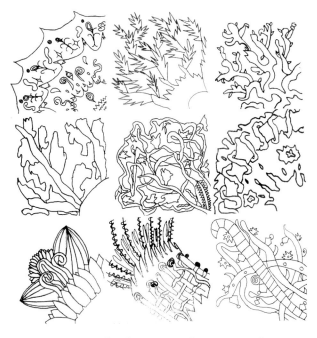

2. Create a design on the 6 x 6-in. sheet that originates from the bottom right corner.

This bottom right corner is diagonally opposite from the letter "A." The design should be reminiscent of plant forms and can be representational or abstract, meaning it could look just like a plant or be a design that is only suggestive of a plant (see student examples above). Use pencil. Turn the finished design over (it should be visible from the back) and trace over it on the back in ink or pencil. This two-sided design will now be the template for creating the 12 x 12-in. design.

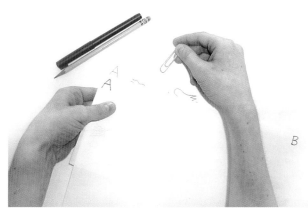

3. Paperclip the two pieces together and trace.

Put the smaller piece behind the larger piece in the upper left corner so that the top "A" is directly on top of the "A" on the sheet underneath it. Use the paperclip to keep the edges aligned and trace with a fine tip permanent marker.

Tip

Keeping the project on a white surface makes it easier to see the lines through the paper when tracing.

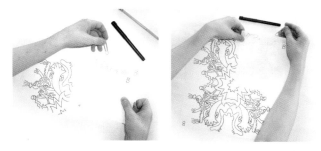

4. Turn the small sheet over and clip to the "B" side.

Once the entire design has been traced, flip the 6 x 6-in. piece over and overlap the "B's" in the upper right corner and trace. This mirror image of the pattern will create new, interesting shapes as lines connect. Rotate the large piece 180 degrees and repeat the first two steps until the entire sheet is filled with the design.

Tip

If a student finds it too difficult to see the pattern through the top sheet when tracing, it may be necessary to outline the 6 x 6-in. pencil drawing in ink on both sides.

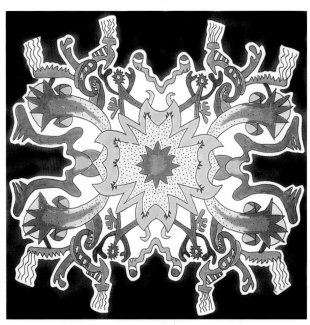

5. Add color to the design.

The permanent black lines will not smudge or run when using watercolors, markers, or colored pencils to fill in the design with color.

6. Cut out the finished design and glue to a 12 x 12-in. piece of black construction paper.

Cut just outside of the edge of the design. This makes it easier to cut around intricate designs and it also creates a nice white border that stands out against the black paper. Glue the project to the black paper.

radial symmetry: a design based on a circle in which both sides are identical and the features radiate from a central point.

a/b pattern: a method used to create radial symmetry.

organic: free-form, or a quality that resembles living things. The opposite of mechanical or geometric.

STUDENT WORK AGES 11-12

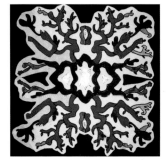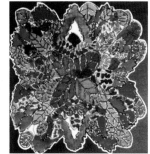

BIRDS OF THE RAIN FOREST

Toucan. © 2005 Getty Images

CONCEPTS

RAIN FOREST
TROPICAL BIRDS
COLLAGE

Tropical rain forests cover only 7% of the world's surface, yet nearly one-half of the world's species of plants and animals are found there. They are unique because of their biodiversity (variety of plant and animal life). Scientists are still discovering new plants, animals, and insects there. These lush green jungles circle the equator in a 3,000-mile-wide belt running through parts of South America, Central America, Southeast Asia, and Africa. About 27 million acres of tropical rain forests disappear each year. In the last 30 years, more than 40% of the world's rain forests have been destroyed. Forty species and 20 acres of rain forest are killed per minute. If this rate of destruction continues, the rain forests and their inhabitants will be gone in less than 50 years. Clearing rain forests has reduced nature's capacity to produce oxygen and added greenhouse gases to the atmosphere. As much as one quarter of the carbon dioxide now in the air was released when rain forests were burned.

Currently the world's richest bird life, over 1,000 species, is found in the Amazon rain forest. Many have exotic plumage in many bright colors. These include parrots, parakeets, toucans, hummingbirds, macaws, and many others.

This project helps to enlighten students to the dilemma of this valuable and fragile resource as well as engage their imagination in creating their own exotic endangered bird (the only one left!) that is found only in the deepest part of the rain forest. A collage of overlapping leaves in the foreground of the picture represents the dense jungle where this fantastic bird makes his home.

MATERIALS

Two 12 x 18-in. sheets bright white construction paper
Pencil
Fine tip permanent marker
Watercolor paints and/or watercolor markers
Tempera paint (blue, yellow, green, red)
Soft round paint brush
Two spray water bottles with dyes (yellow, blue) **(Must be used only by an adult)**
Glue (not pictured)
Scissors

1. Draw a bird.

- Use a pencil to create a big (about 12 inches across) curving line that is like a backward "c" with an extending line at the bottom (body).
- Draw a short slanting line going inward from the top end of the "c" (beak).
- Add another line to that line that goes up until it connects to the "c" to make an enclosed triangle shape (beak).
- Go to the lowest corner of that triangle and draw another line that curves and connects to the bottom tail of the "c" (top of body).
- Go beyond the tail with this curving line four or five inches, then make a tight curve back up to the tail of the "c." Repeat these lines three or four times (tail feathers).
- Lift the pencil and go toward the front bottom of the "c" and add a cluster of three small curving scallops that attach to the "c." Go over about an inch and add one more cluster (feet).
- At the top, to the right of the triangle, draw a smaller circle inside of a bigger circle (eye).
- Next, place the pencil on the lowest corner of the triangle and draw a curving line that goes down and around to make a smaller backward "c" inside of the bigger backward "c" (wing).
- Finish by going to the top of the big "c" and adding a tall curving cluster of scallops or zigzags that attach to the "c" (head feathers).

Using this "script" to describe the drawing process helps children learn how to isolate and analyze bits of visual information in terms of lines and shapes which will help to increase their drawing skills.

Tip

Instruct children to use a light touch with the pencil as they draw. It is much easier to erase mistakes if they are not drawn with heavy bold lines.

2. Draw a vine or tree branch under the bird's feet.

Starting from the left edge of the paper midway down or more, draw a wavy line across the paper up to the tail then stop and continue on the other side up to the first claw or foot of the bird, stop again, then continue on the other side of the foot then continue to the right edge of the paper. Make a parallel line about an inch below the first line.

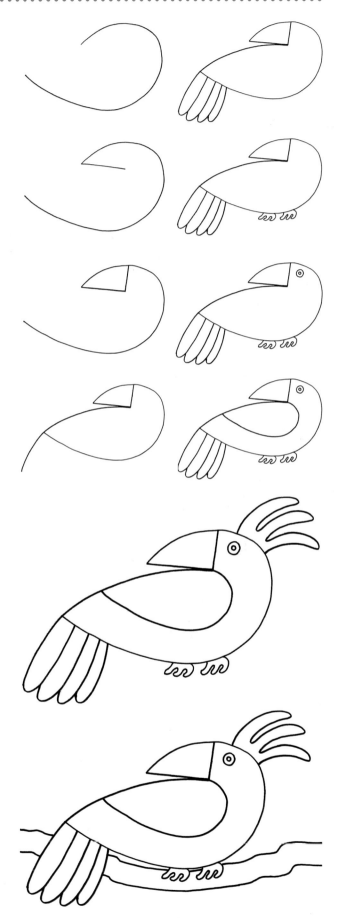

3. Add designs inside the bird drawing.

Using zigzags, wavy lines, straight lines, curving lines, or scalloped lines, each student creates their own individual patterns on the wing, body, head, and tail of this bird drawing. Above are two versions.

4. Color the bird drawing.

Watercolor paints can be mixed to create infinitely more colors than markers alone. If markers are used, adding watercolor paints on top can soften the markers and add interesting color variations.

rain forest: a tropical woodland with an annual rainfall of at least 100 inches and marked by lofty broad-leaved evergreen trees forming a continuous canopy.

tropical birds: colorful birds that live in a rain forest or other region or climate that is frost free with temperatures high enough to support year-round plant growth.

collage: a technique in which an artist glues material such as paper, cloth, or found materials to some type of background.

5. Draw the jungle leaves.

On a separate sheet of 12 x 18-in. white construction paper, draw exotic leaf shapes extending in from all four edges of the sheet again using wavy, zig-zag, and curving lines .

6. Paint the leaves.

Mixing and/or blending the blue, green, red, and yellow tempera paints on each leaf drawing creates interesting color variations. Tempera paint offers intense color against the softer watercolor bird.

7. Outline the bird and leaf paintings.

Use the black permanent marker to trace over all the original pencil lines of the bird and leaf drawings once the paint has dried.

9. Cut out jungle leaves.

Once outlined with the black permanent marker, cut out all the leaves.

8. Add dyes with spray bottles.

Lay out a drop cloth or newspaper, set the bird painting in the center and lightly spray around the bird with the yellow dye. Then add a bit of blue spray. As soon as the blue contacts the yellow, it will turn green. (Optional: make a stencil to cover and protect the bird when spraying)

10. Arrange leaves around the bird and glue in place.

Arrange the leaves around the bird so that they overlap the bird and each other in interesting ways. Glue the leaves in place and trim away any excess leaf parts that extend beyond the paper.

STUDENT WORK AGES 9-10

MATISSE PAPER CUTOUTS

CONCEPTS
COLLAGE
ELEMENTS: SHAPE, COLOR, SPACE
PRINCIPLES: CONTRAST, BALANCE,
MOVEMENT

Henri Matisse,1869-1954. *Beasts of the Sea*, 1950, paper on canvas, 116¹/₈ x 60⁵/₈ in. National Gallery of Art, Washington, DC. Ailsa Mellon Bruce Fund © 2004 Succession H. Matisse / Artists Rights Society (ARS), New York

Henri Matisse (1869-1954) began a career in law in compliance with his father's wishes. He studied law in Paris and passed his law exam with honorable mention then returned home to work in a law office. He found that it was for him boring and mechanical. At age twenty, he suffered appendicitis. While he spent hours in bed recovering, his mother brought him a set of paints, two canvases and two pictures to copy to pass the time. Matisse later said, "The moment I had this box of colors in my hands, I had the feeling that my life was there…. Before, nothing interested me, after that, I had nothing on my mind but painting." Upon his recovery, he began taking art lessons before and after work each day. Eventually he convinced his father to fund a year at an art school. Fellow students nicknamed him "the doctor" because of his horn-rimmed glasses and serious, reflective air. But not apparent to the eye was his capacity to take risks and to persist, against all odds, in his passion for art. His teachers encouraged him to develop his own style. Matisse wished to paint his emotional reaction to a subject rather than its realistic appearance. His brave innovative approach used expressive brush strokes, vivid colors, and flat simplified form. His style sparked a new movement called Les Fauves or the Wild Beasts, a term coined by initially shocked critics. It was the beginning of his long and illustrious career as an artist.

In the early 1950s his health began to fail. To facilitate his creative passion, Matisse began a new direction with his art he called "painting with scissors." Even though he was bedridden, this process enabled him to sit and paint sheets of paper in brilliant colors rather than having to stand at an easel. He then created pictures with this paper by cutting and assembling shapes on canvas with glue. No serious artist had taken this process, called collage (col-*lahj*), to this extreme of description and refinement. He went on to create several famous large-scale "cut outs" over the period of the next ten years. The subject matter came from his imagination invoked through poetry and his life experiences. These collages demonstrated his genius for knowing how elements worked together to make color and shapes come to life.

This project utilizes bright papers, scissors, glue, and the added third dimension to bring this collage to life in the style of Matisse's paper cutouts. Using graduated squares makes the project more fun and easy to create. It also addresses six of the art elements and principles: shape, color, space, contrast, balance, and movement.

collage: a technique in which an artist glues material such as paper, cloth, or found materials to some type of background.

shape: an area that is contained within an implied line or is seen and identified because of color or value changes. Shapes have two dimensions, length and width, and can be geometric or free-form.

color: visual sensation dependent on the reflection or absorption of light from a surface; hue, value, and intensity are the three main characteristics of color.

space: expanse in two- and three-dimensional art which we describe in terms of height, width, and depth; the artwork is divided into positive (the object itself) and negative space (the surrounding area).

contrast: differences in values, colors, textures, and other elements in an artwork to achieve emphasis and interest.

balance: a principle of design that refers to the equalization of elements in a work of art. There are three kinds of balance: symmetrical, asymmetrical, and radial.

movement: a principle of design that refers to the arrangement of parts in a drawing to create a slow to fast flow of your eye through the work.

MATERIALS

Mat board
Mat knife (Must be used only by an adult)
Ruler (not pictured)
Colored paper (8½ x 11 inches in bright colors)
Glue sticks or clear gel glue (not pictured)
Scissors
Foam board (or cardboard or ½ x 24 x 48-in. sheet Styrofoam)

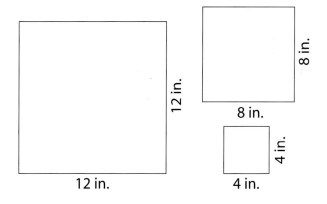

1. Cut three squares of either cardboard or foam board.

Cut with a mat knife and ruler on the mat board in these three sizes.

2. Select, cut, and assemble colored paper shapes on each stacking Styrofoam piece.

Cut large simple shapes of colored paper to cover the base of the 12 x 12-in. foam board piece and to serve as a foundation for the subsequent layers. Use contrasting colors, shapes, and sizes.

Tip

To create more interest, cut wavy, zigzag, and diagonal edges for the papers on the bottom layer of the collage.

3. Stack the second piece of Styrofoam and cover with more cutouts.

Glue the 4 x 4-in. piece of Styrofoam on top of the first and continue adding cut outs.

4. Stack the third piece of Styrofoam and continue covering with cutouts.

5. Using small Styrofoam blocks bits and small shapes add details.

In a few places, small shapes can be raised with Styrofoam blocks glued underneath.

DREAMINGS

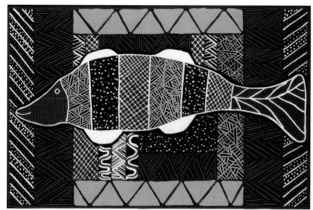

Maryanne Tungatalum, Tiwi (Bathurst/Melville) Clan. *Barramundi*. Gouache on paper, 22 x 34 in. Collection of Tony Haruch. © 2005 Crystal Productions

CONCEPTS
AUSTRALIAN ABORIGINES
DREAMINGS
CULTURAL BELIEF

Throughout the tropical uppermost Northern Territory of Australia, or Arnhem Land, live a dark-skinned people who have inhabited the land for thousands of years. Isolated in a unique and harsh environment, these Aborigines are found not to be closely related to any other people. They have developed a society of clans where everyone is considered kin and subject to the unique beliefs and ceremonial customs that dictate their solutions for a stable and efficient way of life. They believe in what they call a "dreamtime" or a time when the earth first began and their ancestors first created the landscape, plants, animals, and beings that inhabited it. This belief is manifested in unique visual images or paintings called Dreamings. The highly stylized images within the paintings represent the "Dreaming Beings" (or ancestors), their places of travel, habitation, and experiences.

Traditionally, Dreamings were created with human hair brushes and natural pigments from the earth on eucalyptus bark tied to sticks. White and black paint were the most frequently used colors on the surface of the reddish brown bark.

Two distinct styles have developed and lasted for thousands of years. One Dreaming style, from the desert regions employs "shimmering" dots. The other style, from the Arnhem Land territory, uses delicate and detailed line designs. This style is sometimes referred to as the "x-ray" style because of the designs within animal images that symbolize internal organs and skeletal structure.

This project employs both styles and also the new white marker or gel pen that creates a wonderful opaque line on dark paper. The scale of the project was actually determined by this medium.

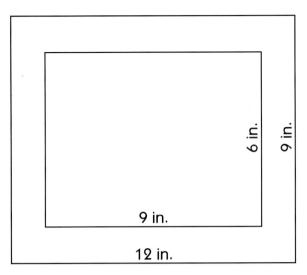

6 in.

9 in.

9 in.

12 in.

MATERIALS

8½ x 11-in. Colored card stock (dark colors – navy blue, burgundy, forest green, dark brown, rust)

Black fine point permanent marker

White marker or gel pen

Tempera paint (white, black)

Paint brush

Glue stick or clear gel glue (not pictured)

9 x 12-in. reddish-brown construction paper

6 x 9-in. white construction paper

Masking tape

Hole punch

Aluminum foil

Aboriginal Dreaming image examples (page 73)

1. Center and glue the 6 x 9-in. white construction paper piece onto the 9 x 12-in. brown piece.

Use a glue stick or clear gel glue to glue the two sheets of paper together.

2. Add dot patterns in the border.

Pour two small puddles of the black and white paint on tin foil or disposable plate. Dip the tip of the paint brush handle into the paint and "dab" the brown border with dot patterns. Dip frequently for uniform dots.

Tip

To avoid smearing paint, rotate the piece away from you as you stamp dots.

3. Tear one or more pieces of card stock to fit within the 6 x 9-in. white piece.

Keeping thumb and index fingers of both hands close together while tearing allows for a more controlled tear along precut shapes.

4. Draw animal Dreamings on each torn piece.

Refer to the examples in this lesson to create similar style animal drawings with pencil then with the black fine tip permanent marker. Make them fit within the torn piece. Large torn pieces might accommodate more than one image. If there are any "mess-ups," simply turn the piece over for a fresh start.

5. Outline the black line drawings with the white gel roller pen.

The delicate white line stands out in contrast against the black marker and dark paper. Draw next to all black lines on one or both sides. Add white dots as well if desired.

6. Optional: create a second border.

Add another border in an Aborigine-inspired pattern inside the dot border with the extra fine tip permanent black marker. Draw it along the edge of the 6 x 9-in. white sheet. Use the six border patterns on page 73 for ideas.

7. Glue torn pieces with finished drawings to the white paper.

Arrange and glue each piece into place with glue stick.

9. Attach sticks or paper twist to project.

Use real sticks or lengths of brown paper twist and attach them with strings of the natural raffia through the holes with square knots. Trim off excess.

8. Reinforce paper and punch holes.

Turn project over and add a piece of masking tape to all 4 corners and half way along two sides to reinforce the paper. Punch ⅛ inch (or ¼ inch) holes within the tape in uniform places along the edge.

Australian aborigines: a member of the indigenous peoples of Australia (the original inhabitants of the continent).

dreamings: stories and paintings of the history and culture of Australia, handed down from generation to generation since the beginning of time (the Dreamtime).

cultural belief: rituals and ceremonies adapted by indigenous groups that define the history of the earth and its inhabitants.

RESOURCES

Australian Aboriginal Paintings by Jennifer Isaacs. This book contains many full color examples with accompanying explanations. 1992 Dutton Studio Books.

VAN GOGH STILL LIFE

Vincent van Gogh, 1853-1890. *Sunflowers*, August 1888. Oil on canvas, 35⁷/₈ x 28 in. (91 x 71 cm). Neue Pinakothek, Munich, Germany. © 2005 Crystal Productions and its Licensors

CONCEPTS

STILL LIFE
IMPASTO
OVERLAPPING
BRAYER

Because of Vincent van Gogh's (1853-1890) letters to his brother, Theo, we have a rare insight into his short, turbulent life that has brought particular meaning to his art. Even though he actually sold only one piece of art, *The Red Vineyard*, during his lifetime, all of his 870 paintings and 1050 drawings are now considered priceless.

He did not begin painting until he was 27 after struggling to find purpose and direction as a minister, teacher, and art dealer. With only a brief period of formal training, he began to paint. His exposure to the Impressionists influenced him to paint with brilliant color. He developed a style of applying this color in thick paint and assertive brushstrokes called *impasto* in which each brush stroke remained defined in a thick application of paint creating a characteristic texture.

Van Gogh expressed strong emotions in his artwork. He suffered mental illness, and he was driven to paint his most brilliant work even during his darkest hours. Sadly, he died at age 37.

This project focuses on one of van Gogh's famous still life paintings, *Sunflowers*. A still life is a picture of a collection of predominantly inanimate objects. This lesson teaches students to draw the horizon line up toward the center, versus the bottom, of the paper, to curve the bottom of the vase giving it a more three-dimensional look, and to overlap shapes (flowers) within the vase. Students also have the opportunity to use a brayer (a rubber roller used to transfer ink in the printmaking process) that adds rich texture against the colorful chalk pastels. Children love the dramatic results.

MATERIALS

12 x 18-in. black construction paper
White glue
Pencil
Colored chalk
Brayer
Black tempera paint

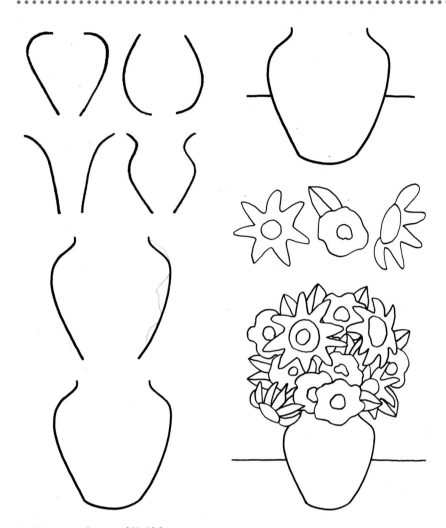

2. Add glue to pencil lines.

Using white glue, add a line of glue over all pencil lines in the picture. Further simplify shapes, if needed, to keep glue lines separate.

1. Draw the still life.

Begin about 3-4 inches from the bottom of the vertical black paper and draw opposing right and left lines that are symmetrical in a shape of your choice from one of the vase shapes above. Connect these two lines at the base with a curved line. Extend horizontal lines from the middle area of the vase to the edge of the paper. This is the top of the table on which the vase sits. At the top of the vase, create flowers by drawing a collection of simplified overlapping "bumpy" circles and zigzags. For leaves, draw two lines that come to a point and include an additional line down the middle. Some lines may overlap the vase. Avoid fine detail.

3. Add colored chalk.

Once the glue has dried and it is clear and hard, add color to the areas inside and outside of the glue using colored chalk. Use a finger to blend and mix color and a damp paper towel to periodically wipe fingers to help keep colors "fresh."

still life: an arrangement of inanimate objects to draw or paint.

overlapping: a perspective technique involving the placement in a flat composition of one object in front of another, creating the illusion of depth.

impasto: thick, heavy application of paint, with either brush or knife.

brayer: a roller used to apply printing ink evenly over the surface of the plate or block. These hand rollers are usually made of rubber of varying degrees of firmness.

Tip

Avoid blowing chalk dust every-where. Instead, work it into the project or tap the edge of the sheet on the table to eliminate any excess.

4. Add black tempera paint.

Dispense a small pool about four inches in diameter of black tempera paint onto a cookie sheet, piece of butcher paper, or the Formica top of a desk. Coat the brayer with the paint by catching just the edge of the puddle with the brayer and rolling down. Roll up and down a few times with this small amount of paint until the brayer is evenly coated. Pull down a little more of the paint when needed.

Roll the brayer over all the glue lines in the picture. Do not be concerned if the brayer leaves unwanted blotches of black paint; they are easy to cover.

5. Eliminate unwanted black areas.

Once the paint has dried, use the chalk to color over any unwanted black paint but be careful not to remove too much.

STUDENT WORK AGES 9-10

PSYCHEDELIC SAND DOLLARS

CONCEPTS

OVERLAPPING
PRINCIPLES: MOVEMENT

This project directs children to take a close look at a little wonder of nature, the sand dollar, and help them appreciate the beauty of its delicate subtle patterns. A drawing lesson illustrates a simplified version of the components of a sand dollar and introduces the concept of overlapping and principle of movement.

A Sand Dollar is really a little sea urchin that is found on the shallow sandy bottoms of the ocean. Its disk-like shape allows it to travel in the currents. Sometimes it is accidentally washed ashore where it's furry covering quickly dries in the sun. Unable to return to the sea, the little animal inside dies leaving behind a beautiful skeleton. It is said that you will find good luck if you find an unbroken sand dollar.

Using bright chalk and glitter on black paper gives a twist to this project that creates something psychedelic or more imaginary in appearance. The proportions of the project are kept small for younger children.

MATERIALS

9 x 12-in. black construction paper (or purple)
Chalk pastels
8½ x 11-in. sheet colored paper (light colors)
Scissors
Glue sticks or clear gel glue (not pictured)
White glue
Gold glitter
Sand dollar

1. Narrate your close observation of a sand dollar while illustrating the details.

- Draw a "bumpy" circle.
- Inside the circle draw a flower with five "fat" petals.
- Draw a skinny flower inside of the fat flower.
- Draw lots of short lines between the flowers.
- Add more short lines all around the inside of the bumpy circle.

Here are examples of some of the fun variations students have come up with on their own:

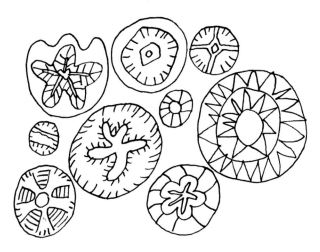

2. Explain and demonstrate overlapping.

Start by drawing two intersecting circles. Then erase one of the intersecting lines within a circle to transform these round lines into two solid objects where one is on top and the other is underneath to create "overlapping."

Return to the original sand dollar drawing and draw another one that is partially hidden behind the first one by extending a horseshoe-shaped line from the edge of the sand dollar.

Finish the details in the new sand dollar and remind students that even the design inside gets overlapped.

3. Begin the project on black paper.

Use the chalk and draw bumpy circles on the black construction paper. Make some overlap and make some go off the edge of the paper so that only part of the sand dollar is left on the page. Since the sand dollar looks like it is leaving or entering the picture plane, it creates a feeling of movement. It suggests to our mind that this position is temporary and change is imminent since the ocean is always moving.

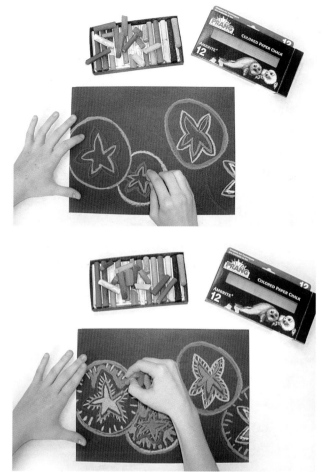

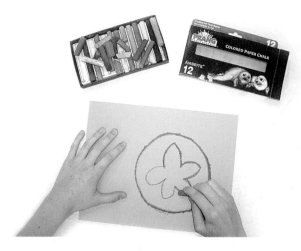

4. Fill in the circles with the sand dollar components.

Use lots of different colors to add lines and fill in shapes with color.

5. Draw and cut out a sand dollar.

On a separate piece of 8½ x 11-in. paper in a bright color (yellow, light orange, pink, lime green, etc.) draw and color one more sand dollar and cut out.

sand dollar: a flat sea urchin that lives in the ocean in shallow water that has a sandy bottom.

overlapping: a perspective technique involving the placement in a flat composition of one object in front of another, creating the illusion of depth.

movement: a principle of design that refers to the arrangement of parts in a drawing to create a slow to fast flow of your eye through the work.

6. Glue the sand dollar to the main composition.

Choose an area along an edge and attach the sand dollar with glue. Let part of the sand dollar extend past the edge of the black paper.

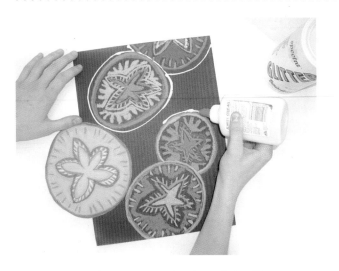

7. Add white glue and gold glitter.

Generally an adult should do this for younger children. Place the tip of the nozzle directly on the paper and draw thin glue lines loosely around the sand dollar shapes. Add small random dots of glue between and on the sand dollars. Sprinkle gold glitter over this catching the excess on a sheet of paper for recycling.

STUDENT WORK AGES 7-9

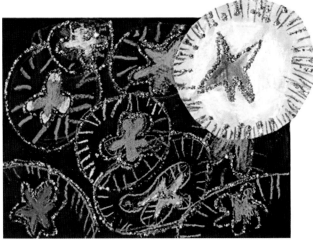

MOLAS

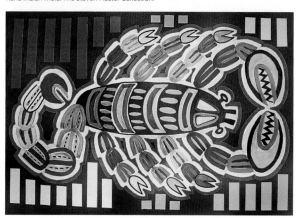

Kuna Indian Mola. The Steven Heater Collection.

CONCEPTS

KUNA INDIANS
MOLAS
APPLIQUÉ

Authentic molas are brightly colored pieces of intricately appliquéd cloth made by the Kuna Indians who live on the San Blas Islands off the east coast of Panama. The Kunas live on approximately 50 of the more than 365 of these islands today. They originally resided in the Panama/Columbia area for centuries. The Spanish explorers encountered them in the 15th century and enslaved and slaughtered thousands, and they introduced European diseases that killed thousands more. The Kunas managed to survive as a people, however, and they learned to trade with the Europeans. By the mid-1800s they began their migration to the Caribbean coast and San Blas Islands to escape jungle disease, weather calamities, and to be closer to the trading ships. The Germans introduced them to brightly colored cloth, scissors, needles, and thread. The first molas began to appear in the late 1800s. Today, the Kuna Indians still lead a tribal life with strong traditions in spite of their daily interaction with the many ships that pass through the canal.

The Kuna women sew as much as they can between the chores of everyday life. Girls are taught to make Molas as early as 4 or 5 years old. A woman, taking great pride in craftsmanship and intricate design, might spend up to 100 hours completing a Mola. Favorite colors are red, yellow, and black. The designs are inspired from observations of the world around them, whether it's a geometric design, vegetation, animal, or man-made object. Today, molas are sold all over the world and because of a well-organized co-op, most of the proceeds return to the Kuna people.

Three types of appliqué are incorporated into a mola. Reverse appliqué is the process where different colored fabrics are layered, then shapes or designs are cut out of the upper layers to reveal the layers below. The raw edges are then delicately turned under and hand-stitched together with thousands of intricate stitches. Overlay appliqué is the process where a cut-out fabric shape is attached on the surface in the same manner. The third process is inlay appliqué which utilizes bits of fabric by sandwiching them in between existing layers to create a wider variety of background colors.

This project incorporates the wonderful traditional mola designs into a bright paper collage.

MATERIALS

12 x 18-in. colored construction paper (black, yellow, red, royal blue)

12 x 18-in. bright white construction paper

Markers (water-based–all colors)

Scissors

Pencil

Glue sticks or clear gel glue (not pictured)

8½ x 11-in. colored paper (bright colors)

Mola patterns (see page 85)

mola: literally clothing, dress, or blouse. Today the term has come to mean the appliqué panels of a Kuna woman's blouse which have gained renown as a distinct form of folk art.

Kuna Indians: Native Indians of Panama who inhabit the Comarca de Kuna Yala which has been a semi-autonomous territory with the country of Panama since 1925. This region consists of more than 365 islands and a strip of land on the Atlantic coast of Panama.

appliqué: a method of decoration in which a motif is cut from one piece of material and attached, or "applied" to another.

1. Draw one large mola shape on the white paper.

Choose one animal or plant or geometric design and make a large pencil drawing. Use the patterns on page 85 for additional ideas.

2. Color 2-3 bands of color around the object.

Use a chisel point marker on its broadside to outline the object. Outline again with a second color.

3. Color in the mola.
Use the waterbase markers to color the drawing in bright colors.

4. Cut out the mola.

5. Add glue to the back of the mola.
Use glue stick.

6. Attach the mola to construction paper and lay out strips of colored paper.
Choose a color of construction paper that will contrast with the mola. A paper cutter is handy but not absolutely necessary for cutting strips of paper. Lay the strips where they will be attached and cut them to fit. Another layer of color could be added to each strip with a marker if desired (see student work on page 84).

7. Glue strips of paper to the mola.
Once all the strips have been cut to size, lift each strip and add glue and attach the strip.

STUDENT WORK AGES 7-8

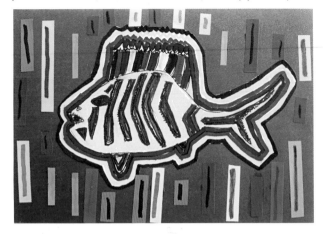

ADDITIONAL TEACHER EXAMPLES

ALPHABET ART

TOPIC
STUART DAVIS
CONCEPTS
ELEMENTS: LINE, SHAPE
ALPHABET LETTERS

This project focuses on the elements of line, shape, and color found in numbers and letters as they connect to each other in an abstract design. Young children readily grasp the idea of connecting letters to make designs and produce amazingly unique patterns on their own. Good, fresh markers help to ensure quality artwork in this project.

The art of Stuart Davis (1894-1964) is the springboard for this project. His father was the art editor for the Philadelphia Press and had contacts with many artists who influenced Stuart. Growing up, his own artistic talents were encouraged and at age 19 were critically recognized in an exhibit. At this time there was little interest in Europe's avant garde (new ideas) but after a visit to Paris, Stuart embraced the modernistic style and philosophies and brought Cubism into American art. He used the forms of his environment, the American city, in his style by creating geometric patterns with intricate flat shapes, numbers, and letters in bright contrasting colors that suggested the zest and rhythm of a billboard, poster, and sign-saturated city life. It was a distinctively American style that reflected the quickened pulse of industrialized America. He was an articulate spokesman for abstract art. He also taught and lectured at several universities and published writings on art theory.

Stuart Davis (1894-1964). *Blips and Ifs*, 1963-1964. Oil on canvas, 71¹/₈ x 53¹/₈ in. 1967.195, Amon Carter Museum, Fort Worth, Texas, Acquisition in memory of John de Menil, Trustee, Amon Carter Museum, 1961-1969

MATERIALS
12 x 18-in. bright white construction paper (or other drawing paper)
Fine tip permanent black marker
Watercolor markers (all colors)

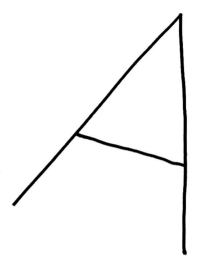

1. Draw a large letter.

Choose a letter from the alphabet and draw it very large on the 12 x 18-in. sheet of white paper with the fine tip black permanent marker. It does not need to be centered or upright.

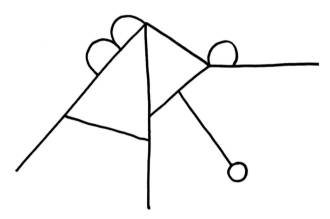

2. Add more connecting letters.

The connecting letters will create new shapes. Letter stories help engage the children's creativity. (e.g., the "B" is sliding down the big "A," "Y" has baby "o" on a leash so it will not run away, letters are marching over the letter mountain, etc.)

Young children enjoy this make-believe but remind them that they are only drawing letters and numbers that connect to each other and not pictures of recognizable things.

3. Fill the page with letter designs.

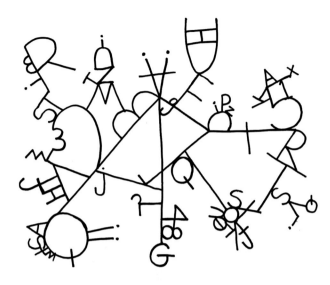

4. Add color.

Everywhere letters connect, new shapes are made. These can be filled with color.

line: the path of a point moving through space; it can vary in width, direction, curvature, length, and even color.

shape: shape is an area that is contained within an implied line or is seen and identified because of color or value changes. Shapes have two dimensions, length and width, and can be geometric or free-form.

letter: a symbol usually written or printed representing a speech sound and constituting a unit of an alphabet.

STUDENT WORK AGES 7-8

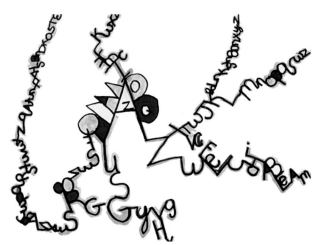

GEOMETRIC MOBILE

TOPIC
ALEXANDER CALDER
CONCEPTS
KINETIC ART: MOBILE
PRINCIPLES: BALANCE, MOVEMENT

Timothy Rose. *Mobile 007*, 2003. Painted sheet metal. 45-in. tall. Courtesy of the artist. www.mobilesculpture.com

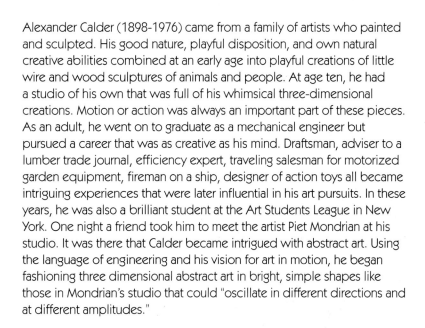

Alexander Calder (1898-1976) came from a family of artists who painted and sculpted. His good nature, playful disposition, and own natural creative abilities combined at an early age into playful creations of little wire and wood sculptures of animals and people. At age ten, he had a studio of his own that was full of his whimsical three-dimensional creations. Motion or action was always an important part of these pieces. As an adult, he went on to graduate as a mechanical engineer but pursued a career that was as creative as his mind. Draftsman, adviser to a lumber trade journal, efficiency expert, traveling salesman for motorized garden equipment, fireman on a ship, designer of action toys all became intriguing experiences that were later influential in his art pursuits. In these years, he was also a brilliant student at the Art Students League in New York. One night a friend took him to meet the artist Piet Mondrian at his studio. It was there that Calder became intrigued with abstract art. Using the language of engineering and his vision for art in motion, he began fashioning three dimensional abstract art in bright, simple shapes like those in Mondrian's studio that could "oscillate in different directions and at different amplitudes."

For the next 45 years, Calder never tired of finding new ways to suspend every conceivable combination of spheres, disks, cones, and other geometrical forms in bright primary colors into dynamic *kinetic* (moving) and unpredictable sculptures called *mobiles*. He produced thousands of unique pieces in the course of his long career. Often he is called the father of this art form. His mobiles still charm all audiences.

To create a balanced yet constantly transforming piece of art, this project uses symmetry with colorful geometric paper forms assembled with multicolored paperclips. Pieces may be precut for younger children. Older children may trace and cut pieces from a pattern or make up their own patterns. Once the pieces are decorated with bright sticky labels, and punched with a few holes, they can be assembled in countless variations. No two are alike. Students will learn that symmetry creates balance if they use identical pairs on either side of central pieces and that shapes that are too wide or delicate will not hold their shape with added weight. Once these creations are set free in the currents, they capture your eye.

MATERIALS

Vinyl paper clips with colorful stripe patterns
Poster board (all colors)
Hole punch (⅛-in. diameter)
Sticky labels (bright colored and/or fluorescent
    circles, rectangles)
Scissors
Geometric patterns (page 92)
Mat knife (Must be used only by an adult)
Metal ruler
Mat board (cutting surface)

mobile: balanced construction suspended
from above with parts which move freely
in air currents or which are motorized.

balance: a principle of design that refers
to the equalization of elements in a work
of art. There are three kinds of balance:
symmetrical, asymmetrical, and radial.

movement: a principle of design that
refers to the arrangement of parts in a
drawing to create a slow to fast flow of
your eye through the work.

1. Trace patterns onto various colors of poster board.

Create patterns like those shown on page 92 or create your own.

2. Cut out pieces.

For accuracy, use a metal ruler and mat knife with a mat board as a cutting surface to cut out all traced pieces.

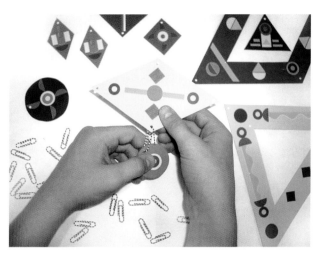

3. Punch holes into each piece.

Use a ⅛-in. hole punch to add holes where pieces will attach to and hang from other pieces. Be careful not to punch too close to the edge or they may tear through.

4. Apply surface designs.

Peel off brightly colored sticky labels and adhere to both sides of each mobile piece in symmetrical patterns. Labels may be modified by cutting into smaller shapes before adhering.

Tip

It helps to wash hands with soap to reduce the natural body oils on finger tips that tend to keep the labels from sticking properly.

5. Assemble mobile.

On a flat surface, experiment with different arrangements before adding paper clips.

The best arrangement is one where all parts hang free of obstruction. Allow about an inch between pieces for the paper clips. Open the paper clip slightly and hook it into a hole and rotate to the first curve, then hook the second piece and close the paper clip.

You may choose to hang fishing line from the ceiling and assemble the mobile in the air. A thumb tack or paper clip, that is inserted in a hung ceiling track, and fishing line is a way to hang the mobile so that it can rotate freely in the air currents.

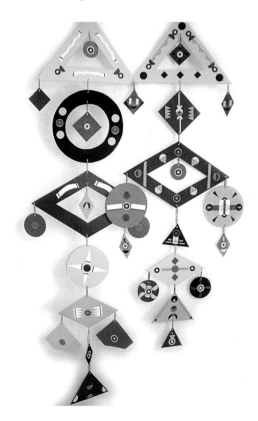

JAZZY JUNGLE CATS

Henri Rousseau, 1844-1910. *Tropical Thunderstorm with a Tiger.* 1891. Oil on canvas. National Gallery, London. Erich Lessing /Art Resource, NY

TOPIC
"JAZZY" CATS

CONCEPTS
ELEMENTS: LINE, SHAPE
OVERLAPPING

A lesson in drawing whimsical lions and fantasy jungles reinforces creativity through use of a variety of lines, shapes, and colors. Each child's cat quickly takes on a personality of its own (e.g., cats wearing socks with different colored toes, cats with big smiles, cats with zigzags, cats that are purple, etc.) Children create a bit of a mystery in this project when they partially hide their cat in giant, overlapping leaves and plants that are reminiscent of French artist Henri Rousseau's jungle paintings like the one above left. Other engaging details might include a bird catching a ride on the back of the cat and/or a snake wrapped in a nearby tree.

Adult involvement in cutting out pieces and working with the child in arranging parts before gluing in place is what brings this project together. Teachers and parents love to frame this art.

MATERIALS
Three 12 x 18-in. sheets of bright white construction paper
Pencil
Black permanent fine tip marker
Scissors
Watercolors
Soft round paint brush
Tempera paints (set of six colors)
Water container
Glue sticks or clear gel glue (not pictured)

1. Draw a cat's body.

Refer to these nine lines and shapes (i.e. straight, zigzag, scalloped, wavy, curving, spiral, heart, spot, and dot) as the building blocks for this drawing. Help students recognize these components in each step. (e.g., the cat's ears are a part of a zigzag line)

 Tip

Instruct children not to press hard on their pencil so they will easily be able to erase parts they don't like.

With a pencil, draw a circle that is about 6 inches in diameter in an upper corner of a 12 x 16-in. sheet of white drawing paper. This will be the cat's head.

Draw another line that connects to the upper part of the circle and curves across the paper and down about 9 inches from the circle.

 Tip

Check students' work at this point. They often draw too small or draw the circle in the center of the paper. If this is the case, they can turn the paper over and try again.

At the end of the curving line, connect another "deep" wavy line that travels back to and connects at the bottom of the circle. Make this wavy line curve up and down four times with a big space between the second and third wave. These are the cat's legs.

2. Add a face and tail to the drawing.

Go to the outside middle part of the big curving line and attach a spiral line for the tail. To complete the tail, draw another spiral inside of it. Connect the two spirals at the end with a zigzag line.

Return to the big circle and draw another circle in the center that is about 3 inches in diameter. This smaller circle will be the cat's face.

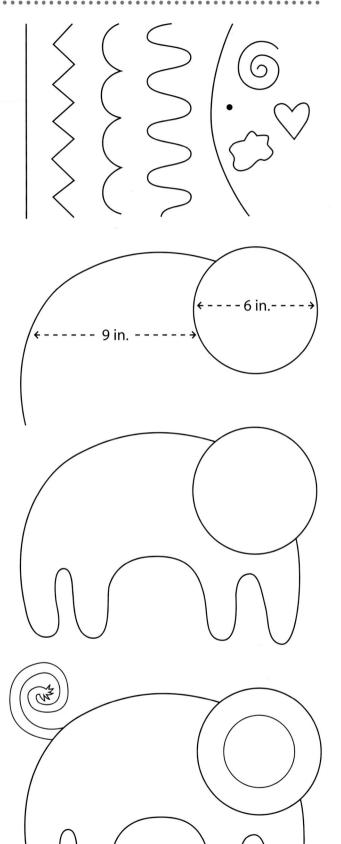

3. Draw the cat's facial features.

- Inside the 3-in. circle draw two small lines that curve up across from each other near the top of the face.

- Connect these two curving lines with one long curved line to make the nose.

- Add two small curved lines to the first two curved lines adding two vertical lines inside to make the eyes.

- Go to the bottom of the cat's nose and draw a horizontal line close to the bottom. Add two dots underneath this line for the cat's nostrils.

- On the very bottom of the nose draw two lines that start in the middle and curve up in opposite directions to form the mouth.

- Attach two pieces of a zigzag line to the top right and left part of the 3-in. circle. Add smaller ones inside of each of these to complete the ears.

- Inside the 3-in. circle, add six dots next to the nose. Put three on the left and three on the right. Draw lines that are about 3-in. long from these dots that extend out and go either diagonally up or down for the whiskers.

4. Decorate the cat.

At this point each child has the framework of a cat to which they can now use their own ideas to add patterns using the nine basic lines and shapes.

5. Paint the cat.

Instruct students to paint the cat's face a fairly light color and to leave the eyes unpainted. Explain that diluting any color with water will make it lighter (e.g., red/pink, purple/lavender, blue/light blue). For other areas of the cat, dark, rich color is achieved when the paint wells have soaked a bit in water before using.

6. Outline the cat and cut out.

Once the cat is dry, trace over all pencil lines with the permanent fine tip permanent black marker. An adult can assist in cutting out the cat. Cut around, not up to, whiskers and/or delicate tails.

line: the path of a point moving through space; it can vary in width, direction, curvature, length, and even color.

overlapping: a perspective technique involving the placement in a flat composition of one object in front of another, creating the illusion of depth.

shape: an area that is contained within an implied line or is seen and identified because of color or value changes. Shapes have two dimensions, length and width, and can be geometric or free-form.

7. Draw jungle plants.

Again using the nine lines and shapes, draw oversized leaves, vines, palms, or other imaginary plants. Above are some typical plant ideas. The leaf on the far left is easiest for younger children.

8. Paint the jungle plants.

Use the tempera paints to paint the plants. Use a mixture of colors rather than just green.

9. Outline and cut out jungle plants.

When the paint is dry, outline over all pencil lines with the fine tip permanent black marker. An adult could cut out all pieces.

10. Assemble cat and jungle together and glue into place.

On a third piece of 12 x 18-in. paper, arrange the pieces. Some pieces will look best behind the cat, others will overlap the cat. Children enjoy testing out various solutions. Glue down with a glue that will not warp the paper. Trim off any pieces that extend beyond the paper.

STUDENT WORK AGES 7-9

GUSTAV KLIMT CRAZY QUILT

Gustav Klimt, Austrian, 1862-1918. *Baby (Cradle)*, 1917/1918. Oil on canvas, 43⅝ x 43½ in. (110.9 x 110.4 cm). National Gallery of Art, Washington, DC. Gift of Otto and Franciska Kallir with the help of the Carol and Edwin Gaines Fullinwider Fund, 1978.41.1

CONCEPTS

ART NOUVEAU

MOTIF

TINT

Gustav Klimt (*Goo-stahv Kleemt*) (1862-1918) was born near Vienna, Austria. His father was an engraver and carver. Klimt's own artistic talent was quickly recognized during his school years. Even though his family was poor, he began attending the School of Arts and Trades of Vienna at age 14. During his seven years there, he learned many diverse techniques from mosaics to fresco. Eventually his own ideas began to conflict with the conservative academic school. A new movement called Art Nouveau was beginning to emerge and Klimt played a key role. This style of art sought to convey the feelings or attitudes of the artist or the social and political concerns of the time. It also called attention to the process of art itself or "art for art's sake." Art Nouveau rejected Renaissance perspective space in favor of motifs that emphasized the flat plane of the composition. It used a style that was based on stylized plant forms and the free-flowing lines of nature. Klimt's paintings have an interesting combination of modeled three-dimensional looking human figures surrounded by flat two-dimensional swirling designs. He also developed a kind of Klimt language with his own unique designs or motifs.

This project utilizes these motifs in a quilt composition that takes its idea from Klimt's painting in 1918 called *Baby* in which a small child rests beneath a quilt of swirling planes of pattern and color. A lesson in color tinting, as seen in *Baby*, is also incorporated into this project. Children enjoy the discovery process of tinting (mixing white with color) to help to create a flat, opaque appearance needed for this Klimt style.

MATERIALS

12 x 18-in. bright white construction paper
Pencil
Watercolors
White "cake" tempera (¾ x 2¼-in. dry cake of tempera paint)
Brush
Motif examples (page 100)
Water
Water container

1. Draw a face.

Position the paper vertically and go to the top third section of the sheet to begin with a face. Discuss and demonstrate first, on another sheet of paper or on a blackboard, the components of a face (e.g. the types of lines used, placement of parts, overlapping shapes, facial expressions) that they may choose to use. Include pets in this discussion as well. Part of the quilt can overlap the face by drawing lines across any part of the head drawing and erasing any lines that extend outside of that line. Above are examples.

Facial parts to be discussed include: open eyes, tired eyes, closed eyes, eyes with eyelashes, eyes that show a pupil, retina and "white part," bushy eyebrows, thin eyebrows, high or low eyebrows, ears, noses straight on and ¾ view, upper and lower lips, lips that smile, big lips, small lips, expressionless lips, chins under the quilt, chins over the quilt, heads that are wide or narrow, heads on pillows, hair types-curly, straight, long, short, bangs, pig tails, crew cuts, sleeping dogs, cats, hamsters, etc. The more possibilities you suggest, the more you stimulate creativity.

2. Draw the quilt sections.

Once the face and head are drawn, a "skeleton" structure of the quilt is made by drawing long diagonal wavy lines that cross over each other and extend to the edges of the paper from the face or faces. These intersecting lines create the quilt sections.

Art Nouveau: an exaggeratedly decorative style which spread through Europe in the last two decades of the 19th century and the first decade of the 20th century. It makes use of undulating forms of all kinds, particularly curving plant stems, flames, waves, and flowing hair.

motif: the underlying idea, the dominant theme, or the distinctive element of design found in a work of art.

tint: lightening of a hue made by adding color to white.

3. Add designs to quilt.

In each section draw different designs using the Klimt motifs (e.g. swirls, squares, "bumpy circles," etc.) See motif examples below and at right.

4. Paint the drawing.

Demonstrate tinting by mixing different watercolors right on the surface of the dry white tempera cakes. Students will see that the more the color is mixed with the white tempera, the lighter it becomes. Demonstrate making skin colors by mixing red, green, yellow, or white, brown, and orange together. Show how two or three colors may be mixed on the watercolor tray before adding white to create really unique colors. Students can experiment on a separate piece of paper.

5. Outline the finished painting.

Once the paint is dry, use a permanent black marker to outline all original pencil lines, even those that may have been partially covered with paint. This helps to emphasize the Klimt motifs, facial details, and give it a more finished look.

Tip

Occasionally a child will "mess up" their face (e.g., skin too dark, smeared lips) after they have beautifully painted the quilt. All is not lost. Cut the face portion out either along the hair line or quilt line depending upon the child's composition and replace with a clean scrap of paper from behind the opening. Tape or glue the piece into place and they can try again.

STUDENT WORK AGES 9-11

DRAGONS IN CAVES

Chris Achilleos. *Dragonspell*. Courtesy of the artist. www.chrisachilleos.co.uk

TOPICS

MIDDLE AGES
DRAGON FOLKLORE
CAVES

In the Bible, Michael and his angels fought against the dragon, "that old serpent, also called the Devil and Satan," and drove him out from Heaven. In Medieval Europe, dragons existed as religious symbols of wickedness in the Christian world, especially the sins of paganism or sins of worldly pleasures that violated religious law. Saints were often pictured in the act of slaying dragons. Christianity conquering sin is symbolized in the legend of Saint George where his success in killing a ferocious dragon to which terrified pagans had been sacrificing a maiden each year, caused them all to become Christians.

These mythical creatures were depicted as enormous reptilian beasts with snake-like bodies, scales, bat-like wings, a spiked spine, claws, horns, barbed tails, fangs, forked tongues, breathing fire and poisonous vapors, and residing in the depths of the earth.

This project utilizes water poured over carbon paper ink to achieve a luminous, dreamlike cavern for a fantasy dragon composition. Most 6th grade curriculum includes a study of the Middle Ages in Europe. This is a creative addition to that unit.

MATERIALS

Two 12 x 18-in. sheets bright white construction paper
12 x 18-in. sheet of black construction paper
Pencil
Scissors
8½ x 11-in. carbon paper
Watercolors
Paint brush
Water container
Glue sticks or clear gel glue (not pictured)

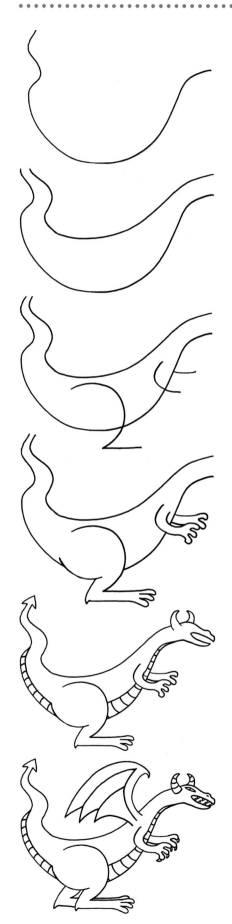

1. Draw a dragon.

- Using a pencil and one 12 x 18-in. sheet of white drawing paper, draw a wavy line that starts high, curves down then up again and ends with another smaller wave. This line extends about 10 inches across the paper. See examples at left.

- Next draw another line above the first that curves in a similar fashion but is wider in the center.

- Inside the widest part, draw a half circle that attaches to a short horizontal line at its base.

- Add two more short curving lines in the upper right. One of these lines crosses over a line and the shorter one ends at the line. These are the arms of the dragon.

- Add parallel lines to all these lines, except the semicircle where the line curves in the opposite direction. Erase lines inside these parallel lines. Enclose each set of parallel lines with a set of small wavy lines to make the dragon's fingers and toes.

- At the upper left of the drawing, extend, then enclose the parallel lines to create a barb on the tail. At the upper right, draw a line that curves down and around inside of itself and back out to form the head and mouth.

- Add two pairs of pointed curving lines at the top (horns). Erase the lines inside and add a series of small curving lines. Add the under-belly "scales" with one long curving line and short lines that attach at intervals.

- Just above the arms, draw three lines that curve up. Erase the lines inside. Attach more lines that curve down and create points (wings). Add a second leg. Add claws, eyes, teeth, and a nostril.

- Finishing details include adding a long wavy zigzag line (representing spikes on back), randomly scattered clusters of small curving lines (scales), and a series of pointed, scalloping lines at the open mouth that twist and connect (fire).

2. Paint the dragon.

Watercolor paints produce an unlimited variety of colors, especially when one color is blended into another as shown here with green and yellow and purple and magenta. This gradation also creates a modeling effect to make the dragon look more three-dimensional.

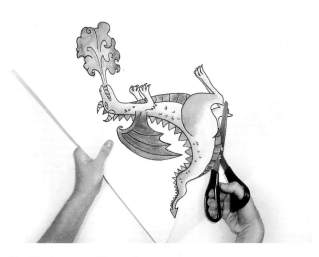

4. Cut out the dragon.

White paper can be left and filled in with the black marker in detailed or enclosed areas. (These areas will blend in with the black background of the cave later on.)

3. Outline the dragon.

Use a fine tip permanent black marker to trace over all pencil lines.

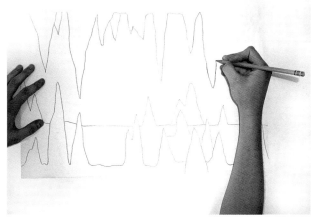

5. Draw the cave.

With a new sheet of 12 x 18-in. paper, draw a series of peaks and valleys along the top of the paper (stalactites) and along the bottom of the paper (stalagmites). Styles vary (straight to wavy, simple to complex).

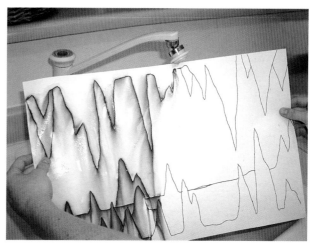

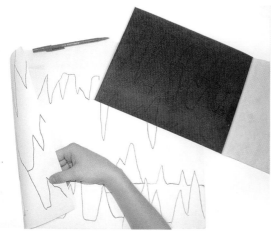

7. Run water over the drawing.

Turn the water faucet to a slow, steady stream and run the ink side of the cave drawing through the water. Lay this sheet flat to dry.

Tip

Cleanser with bleach will remove any sink stains.

6. Add ink lines.

Place the carbon paper, ink side up, under the cave drawing and trace over all lines pressing hard enough to get a good transfer of ink to the reverse side of the drawing. Move the carbon paper as each section is traced until ink is transferred to the entire back of the drawing. Double check for missed areas.

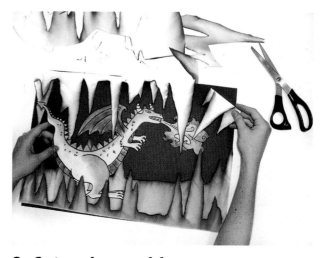

middle ages: the period in Western history between antiquity and the Renaissance, from about 476 to 1453, characterized by feudalism (rule by independent warlords and a subjected peasantry) and the dominance of the Catholic Church.

dragon: a mythical animal usually represented as a monstrous winged and scaly serpent with a crested head and enormous claws.

cave: a natural underground chamber or series of chambers open to the surface.

8. Cut and assemble.

On a 12 x 18-in. black sheet of construction paper, assemble cave parts in front of and behind the dragon. Glue into place.

Optional: run a thin stream of white glue along one side of every stalactite and stalagmite and sprinkle with fine white iridescent glitter to create a sparkle that gives the look of ice.

STUDENT WORK AGES 11-12

BODACIOUS BUGS

E. A. Seguy. *Insects*. © 2005 Dover Publications and its Licensors.

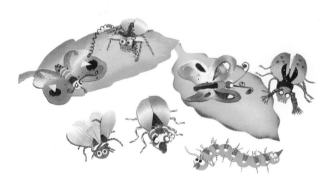

TOPIC
INSECTS

Mention bugs to kids and you gain their instant attention. They are creepy, crawly, repulsive, beautiful, and fascinating creatures. For sheer variety and abundance, they rank among the most successful animals on Earth. About one million species of insects have been identified so far, which is about half of all the animals known to science. Insects have adapted to every habitat in a variety that is amazing. For example, a relative of crickets, called rock crawlers, survive in the peaks of the Himalayas by producing a kind of antifreeze that keeps them from freezing solid. And then there are ants that survive in the center of the Sahara Desert. The Dwarf Beetle measures only 1/100 of an inch long. The Southeast Asian Walkingstick grows to 20 inches long. The heaviest insect in the world, the African Goliath beetle, weighs as much as a small bird.

All insects have six legs, two antennae, a head, thorax, and abdomen. An insect's skeleton is on the outside of its body (called exoskeleton). It is made of a plastic-like material covered with a wax that keeps their organs inside from drying out. Insects are relatively small because they would not be strong enough to carry their exoskeleton around if it was any larger. Insects gather most of their information from their antennae. Some use antennae for sound but most insects use them to smell. Insects have compound eyes that range from poor to keen vision. Insects have blood but it is not red, and they breathe oxygen.

Insects may be regarded as pests because some bite, sting, spread disease, or eat crops, but without insects we would also starve. Crops that we rely on for food require pollination by insects. In many countries, insects themselves are food! Silk, shellac, and honey come from insects. Beneficial insects control harmful insects. Insects help to recycle organic materials and give us nitrogen and other important nutrients.

Entomologists, the name of the people who study insects, consider them to be among the most important and beautiful of all creatures. This project employs a child's creativity in constructing their own "bodacious" bug (beetle, butterfly, or other insect) using aluminum cans, spray paint, vinyl-covered wire, and modeling compound.

MATERIALS

Modeling compound (red, white, yellow, blue, green, black, or a box of assorted colors)

Empty aluminum cans

Fluorescent spray paint (pink, yellow, green, blue) **(Must be used only by an adult)**

Black and/or dark purple spray paint (Must be used only by an adult)

Vinyl covered wire (all colors – art supply catalogs or electrical wiring from hardware stores)

Silicon glue (or other vinyl or metal adhesive)

Aluminum flashing (a roofing material – comes in rolls in 6-, 8-, 10-, 12-in. widths at lumber stores)

Lightweight tin snips

Scissors

Ball point pen

Pencil

Paper 8½ x 11 inches

Mat knife (Must be used only by an adult)

Permanent black fine tip marker

Tip

A flat piece of aluminum can metal is thin enough to safely handle and to cut with scissors, yet sturdy enough to keep its shape when inserted into the polymer clay.

1. Cut open aluminum cans.

- **Adult:** Lay the can on its side and pierce the can just below the top with the mat knife. Rotate the can while "slicing" through the metal until the top is cut off.

  Note: tipping the mat knife slightly to one side eliminates friction in the sawing motion.

- Do the same at the base of the can to remove the bottom. Scissors can finish the last bit of the job once the can has been started with the mat knife.

- Cut down the side of this open cylinder with scissors, uncurl it, and rub it over the edge of a surface to make it lay flat.

- Cut off any ragged edges so that all sides are smooth.

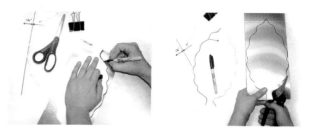

4. Trace the leaf and cut out.

Position the leaf on the metal flashing and trace around it with the permanent marker. Use the tin snips to cut the leaf out.

5. Add veins to the metal leaf.

Press down with a ball point pen to emboss the leaf with a pattern of leaf veins.

2. Spray the metal with paint.

Center the pop can piece, printed side down, on a covered surface and spray with the fluorescent paints in rainbow patterns and/or spatters (paint will spatter if the nozzle is barely depressed). Practice on paper first for the right touch. Black and/or purple paint creates a striking contrast against these fluorescent colors.

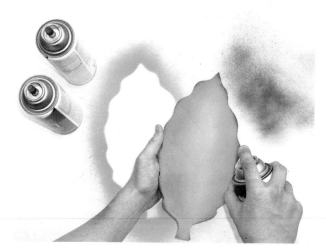

3. Make a leaf pattern.

Fold an 8½ x 11-in. piece of paper in half lengthwise. Draw a line 3 inches from the fold and draw a leaf pattern within that line so that the finished unfolded leaf fits on the 6-in. wide aluminum flashing (unless you are working with a wider piece of aluminum).

6. Spray paint the leaf.

Spray fluorescent yellow in the center, then fluorescent green over the remaining area. Add a touch of dark blue around the edge of the leaf.

7. Make the insects.

Use the modeling compound to create a head, thorax, and abdomen in any combination of colors by making three smooth balls and attaching them in a row. For a butterfly, leave the one for the head round, the middle one elongated slightly for the thorax, and a most elongated one at the end for the abdomen.

9. Cut small shapes in contrasting colors and glue to wings.

Cut and bend vinyl covered wire at one end into a spiral for antennae and proboscis (mouth). Make two small balls of clay for eyes, attach to the head, and pierce each with a pencil for the center of the eye. Insert all parts into the clay.

If needed, prop the wings up slightly underneath while the clay dries and sets.

8. Make and attach wings, antennae and proboscis.

Draw a freehand wing shape on the back of one end of the painted pop can metal with the permanent black marker and cut out. Flip it over and cut a duplicate wing from the first wing on the opposite end of the metal. Do the same with the remaining metal in the center for two more wings.

insect: any of a class of arthropods (bugs, bees, etc.) with a well-defined head, thorax, and abdomen, only three pairs of legs, and typically one or two pairs of wings.

entomologist: a person who studies the life cycles, behavior, ecology, or diversity of insects as their work or hobby.

10. Cut out beetle wings, antennae and six legs.

Twist colored wire together then cut into six matching lengths for legs. Bend the legs into a stair step shape and attach by "pushing" them into the abdomen, three on each side. Use two single wires or pieces of pop can for the antennae and insert these into the top area of the head. Attach wings into the thorax. Add any other finishing details (e.g., spots, stripes, teeth.)

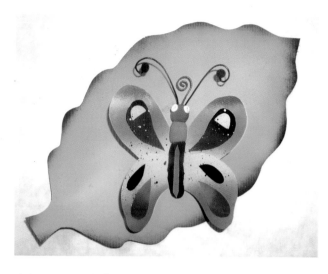

11. Attach insects to the leaf.

The leaf creates a nice backdrop for the insects.
Attach insects with silicon glue and let dry.

CREATE MORE BUGS!

The possibilities are limitless. Other body details might include multiple eyes, a horned nose, hair, spots, spikes, ornate antennae, longer legs, etc. Here are a few more examples.

Glossary

a/b pattern: a method used to create radial symmetry.

abstract art: art which depicts subject matter with simplified or symbolic forms.

appliqué: a method of decoration in which a motif is cut from one piece of material and attached, or "applied" to another.

Art Nouveau: an exaggeratedly decorative style which spread through Europe in the last two decades of the 19th century and the first decade of the 20th century. It makes use of undulating forms of all kinds, particularly curving plants, flames, waves, and flowing hair.

astronomy: the study of objects and matter outside the earth's atmosphere and of their physical and chemical properties.

Australian aborigines: a member of the indigenous peoples of Australia (the original inhabitants of the continent).

balance: a principle of design that refers to the equalization of elements in a work of art. There are three kinds of balance: symmetrical, asymmetrical, and radial.

blending: combining or mixing colors in a work of art to create a smooth transition between colors.

brayer: a roller used to apply printing ink evenly over the surface of the plate or block. These hand rollers are usually made of rubber of varying degrees of firmness.

cave: a natural underground chamber or series of chambers open to the surface.

cityscape: a picture representing a view of urban elements, such as buildings.

clay: a mud-like sediment composed of very fine particles of minerals. Pliable when moist, but becomes hard when dry or fired.

collage: a technique in which an artist glues material such as paper, cloth, or found materials to some type of background.

color: visual sensation dependent on the reflection or absorption of light from a surface; hue, value, and intensity are the three main characteristics of color.

contour drawing: a single line drawing which defines the outer and inner forms (contours) of people or objects.

contrast: differences in values, colors, textures, and other elements in an artwork to achieve emphasis and interest.

cultural belief: rituals and ceremonies adapted by indigenous groups that define the history of the earth and its inhabitants.

dragon: a mythical animal usually represented as a monstrous winged and scaly serpent with a crested head and enormous claws.

dreamings: stories and paintings of the history and culture of Australia, handed down from generation to generation since the beginning of time (the Dreamtime).

entomologist: a person who studies the life cycles, behavior, and ecology of insects.

impasto: thick, heavy application of paint, with either brush or knife.

fantasy space art: art that combines science and our knowledge of the universe to portray imaginary planets and galaxies, landscapes, cities, and civilizations.

faux finish: a decorative paint technique that imitates a pattern found in nature, such as marble or wood.

folk art: regional handicrafts and ornamental works created by people with no formal art training but trained in traditional techniques often handed down through generations.

incise: to engrave or carve into a surface.

insect: any of a class of arthropods (bugs, bees, etc.) with a well-defined head, thorax, and abdomen, only three pairs of legs, and typically one or two pairs of wings.

Kuna Indians: Native Indians of Panama who inhabit the more than 365 islands of the Comarca de Kuna Yala region in Panama.

landscape: a work of art that uses inland natural scenery as subject matter.

letter: a symbol usually written or printed representing a speech sound and constituting a unit of an alphabet.

line: the path of a point moving through space; it can vary in width, direction, curvature, length, and even color.

middle ages: the period in Western history between antiquity and the Renaissance, from about 476 to 1453, characterized by feudalism and the dominance of the Catholic Church.

mobile: balanced construction suspended from above with parts which move freely in air currents or which are motorized.

mola: literally clothing, dress, or blouse. Today the term has come to mean the appliqué panels of a Kuna woman's blouse which have gained renown as a distinct form of folk art.

motif: the underlying idea, the dominant theme, or the distinctive element of design found in a work of art.

movement: the arrangement of parts in a drawing to create a slow to fast flow of your eye through the work.

negative space: area around objects in a work of art; in a two-dimensional work of art, sometimes called the background.

nonobjective art: art which has no recognizable subject matter. The real subject matter is the composition of the drawing or painting itself.

organic: free-form, or a quality that resembles living things. The opposite of geometric.

overlapping: a perspective technique in a flat composition in which one object is placed in front of another, creating the illusion of depth.

pattern: elements repeated over and over, arranged in a predetermined sequence.

petroglyph: a carving or inscription on rock.

printmaking: the art of making works of art from one of the four printmaking processes – relief, intaglio, lithography, and serigraphy.

radial symmetry: a design based on a circle in which both sides are identical and the features radiate from a central point.

rain forest: a tropical woodland with an annual rainfall of at least 100 inches and marked by tall leafy trees forming a continuous canopy.

reflection: transformation which produces the mirror image of an object.

relief: the raised parts of a surface which are often noticeable by the feeling of texture.

repoussé: metal that is shaped or ornamented with patterns in relief made by hammering or pressing on the reverse side.

rhythm: the regular repetition of particular aspects of a design.

salting: sprinkling grains of salt into wet water-color to create texture.

sand dollar: a flat sea urchin that lives in the ocean in shallow water with a sandy bottom.

shape: an area that is contained within an implied line or is seen and identified because of color or value changes. Shapes have two dimensions, length and width, and can be geometric or free-form.

slab method: refers to a ceramic process in which the artist assembles an artwork by hand using flat slabs of clay that have been rolled to a consistent thickness.

space: expanse in two- and three-dimensional art which we describe in terms of height, width, and depth; the artwork is divided into positive (the object itself) and negative space (the surrounding area).

sponging: dipping a sponge in watercolor and stamping it on paper to create texture.

stamping: a technique in which paint or ink is applied to an image that has been carved onto a soft block and then pressed onto any type of media to transfer the image to the media.

still life: an arrangement of inanimate objects to draw or paint.

texture: the surface quality, both simulated and actual, or artwork.

tint: lightening of a hue made by adding color to white.

tropical birds: colorful birds that live in a rain forest or other region or climate that is frost free with temperatures high enough to support year-round plant growth.

watercolor wet-in-wet: adding a watercolor-loaded brush to the wet surface of a paper.

watercolor glazing: the technique of applying a transparent watercolor wash over a dried color area to achieve luminosity and richness.